HOW TO
SURVIVE
—IN THE—
MINISTRY

HOW TO
SURVIVE
—— IN THE ——
MINISTRY

Leslie B. Flynn

KREGEL PUBLICATIONS
Grand Rapids, Michigan 49501

Unless otherwise indicated, scripture quotations are from the Authorized King James Version. Those marked:

NIV are from the New International Version of the Bible, published by the Zondervan Corporation, © 1978 by the International Bible Society.

TLB are from The Living Bible, © 1973 by Tyndale House Publishers, Wheaton IL.

PHILLIPS are from The New Testament in Modern English translated by J.B. Phillips, © 1972 by J.B. Phillips, published by the Macmillian Company, New York, NY.

Cover Photo & Design: Art Jacobs
Book design: Al Hartman

Library of Congress Cataloging-in-Publication Data
Flynn, Leslie B.
How to Survive in the Ministry / Flynn, Leslie B.
    p.   cm.
1. Pastoral theology. 2. Clergy—Office.
3. Flynn, Leslie B. I. Title.
BV4011.F58   1992   253'.2—dc20   91-21652
                                            CIP

ISBN 0-8254-2637-5

1 2 3 4 5 Printing/Year 96 95 94 93 92

Printed in the United States of America

To our friends
of many years

BILL and ALICE BREEDING

Contents

PREFACE

Forty years as pastor of the same church!

On the third Sunday of February, 1949, I preached my first sermon as pastor of Grace Conservative Baptist Church of Nanuet, N.Y., located an hour's drive from Times Square. Forty delightful years later, on the third Sunday of February, 1989, I preached my final sermon and retired from the active pastorate.

Forty years is a long time!

Forty years without fireworks, though not without flare-ups.

Long pastorates are a rarity today. The average length of a pastor's stay has been estimated at around three to four years. According to church administrative experts, this is an insufficient period to build an effective ministry. They claim that a pastor does not really become pastor till at least after five years.

Increasingly, in recent years, pastors have been changing churches, or leaving the ministry. The reasons given are many. When the going gets tough, somehow the grass on the other side of some distant parish fence looks greener. Failing to reach high expectations, a pastor may become deeply discouraged. Thwarting a church dictator, or displeasing an influential clique, may precipitate a series of circumstances beyond a pastor's control, ending in his resignation. Sometimes a pastor's ineptitude brings about his own downfall. Churches are firing pastors in unprecedented numbers. Also, some denominational leaders do not recommend long pastorates, believing change beneficial to both pastor and people. Then, too, some ministers have the gift of taking over a failing congregation, leading it to renewal, then moving on in a few years to another similar challenge.

The sovereign Head of the church does not will every pastor to stay a long time in the same pulpit. Before my forty-year stay at Nanuet I served an enjoyable and contented four-and-a-half year stint in a Pennsylvania mining town. This ended when I accepted a totally unsolicited call to my new field. Generally, however, a short pastorate may rob both pastor and church because the pastor does not "stay by the stuff" long enough to see the church through to new heights of vigor and growth.

How does a pastor survive the stresses of pastoring a church today when perhaps the pastorate is tougher than it's ever been? I do not profess to have even a majority of the answers. But in my review of these last four decades of ministry in this same church several principles stand out. Dialogue with several long-time church members and pastoral friends has confirmed and augmented this list of policies.

This book is not an exhaustive list of survival techniques. Nor is it a manual on pastoral leadership or church management. Nor do I wish to convey the impression that survival should be a pastor's all-consuming passion and highest goal. Rather, this volume is the account of one pastor's methods of ministry, heavily laced with personal experiences, which have contributed to his staying put for forty years. Throughout the text I use the generic "he" to refer to the pastor, but the lessons I've learned are equally applicable to women in the ministry as well.

What may work for one pastor in a particular situation may not fit the personality of another pastor, nor the character of another church. This is the story of what worked for me and the faithful body of Christ in Nanuet, N.Y.

How may a pastor stay forty years in one pulpit? Ultimately, through the goodness of God and the support of a kind congregation.

1

It's Tough to Be a Pastor Today!

It's tough to be a pastor today!

Perhaps tougher than it's ever been!

To begin with, pastors have always seemed vulnerable to certain temptations. Some years ago, before the Christian and Missionary Alliance started its excellent Alliance Theological Seminary at Nyack, N.Y., Nyack Missionary College offered a five-year B.Th. program for students headed for the ministry. As a neighboring pastor of a growing church, I was invited to teach a one-semester course in Pastoral Methods. During the dozen years I led this seminar, sometimes entitled "Pastoral Problems," I always devoted an early session to a discussion of the perils of the ministry.

PITFALLS OF THE MINISTRY

Sexual Indiscretion

Recognizing that clergy sex offenders represent a serious social and ethical issue, *Newsweek* (8/28/89) titled its two-page *Religion* section, "When a Pastor Turns Seducer." The article gives a general portrait of the minister most likely to stray. He is usually middle-aged, disillusioned with his calling, neglecting his own marriage, a lone ranger isolated from clergy colleagues, who meets a woman who needs him and who perceives him as a god-like figure.

To help avoid compromising situations some churches have rules on counseling members of the opposite sex. Some require a third party present, or a partly open door. The best prevention is for a minister to spend more time improving his own marriage.

Biblical models indicate that the sexual problem has been present throughout history. King David's adultery brought disastrous con-

sequences on his family. Solomon's preoccupation with the fair sex
produced his downfall. Church leaders must simply and immediately say no to sexual temptation, lest they become castaways
(1 Cor. 9:7).

Money

No one in his right mind enters the ministry to make money. But
even when poorly paid, a pastor may have the wrong attitude,
envying ministers and members who make more, hinting for higher wages, seeking churches that pay more, or misusing what he
has.

Jesus taught that a close relationship exists between the way we
handle our material possessions and the level of our spiritual tem-
perature. We fool ourselves if we think that we would handle our
finances better if we had more. If we squander a small income
now, we would probably waste a higher salary later. If we handle a
small paycheck wisely now, the Lord may well entrust us with a
higher bracket later on.

The financial scandals of a few TV evangelists with their lavish
spending warn us against becoming careless in money matters.
Pastors must constantly guard against letting the legitimate desire
for more swell into covetousness.

Laziness

Usually no one checks on the hours a preacher devotes to his
job. He doesn't punch a time clock, nor sign in and out of the work-
place, especially if his study is at home. If his office is at church, he
may claim on late arrival that he was working at home, when he
was really watching television. Visitation, whether hospital or home,
provides ample time to lounge and loaf, and linger on personal
errands and conversation.

Alexander Whyte, famed preacher of Edinburgh, considered la-
ziness to be the one unpardonable sin in ministers. When Moderator
of the Presbyterian Assembly in 1898, he admonished the pastors
to major in humility, prayer and work. Pastors need to check on
themselves regularly and vigorously.

Prefessionalism

At a train station one morning a lady sat hunched over the
steering-wheel of her car, looking bewildered. A bystander, approaching her open window, asked, "Are you all right?" The
lady-driver replied, "For fourteen years I've driven my husband to
the station to catch the 7 A.M. train. Today I forgot him!"

How easy to go through the motions without feeling. To talk about the crucifixion sufferings, and to do it casually. To speak of the glorious, triumphant resurrection, without excitement. To visit the sick and sorrowing, to conduct weddings and funerals, to lead services, to preach, all as a mere matter of fact. To stand at the door and greet people perfunctorily. I heard of one minister at the back of the church who kept saying, as one by one his people shared bits of pleasant news, "That's good." Even when a brokenhearted woman whispered, "My son was badly injured in a motorcycle accident last night," he found himself repeating in a hollow, formal voice, "That's good."

For the sake of others the pastor needs to maintain his own spiritual health. Because his vocation is so linked to his spiritual condition, he must constantly beware of professionalization. He must not let his constant use of the Bible rob him of his respect for the Scriptures and his need of obedience to their precepts. He must be careful in prayer lest he be just mouthing words. How deadening to deal with the surface of the sacred. Superficial familiarity breeds contempt.

Pride

The pastor is always up front, the center of attention. This feeds his pride. At the door at the close of the service most everybody tells him how good his sermon was. "I could have listened all day," someone says. Believing the flattery, next Sunday the minister preaches well into the afternoon.

The pastor wants to succeed, be known as the minister of the church with the fastest growing Sunday school, or most active youth group, or largest missionary budget, or biggest evening service. One observer noted that at the local clergy meeting, the same question always surfaced, "How many did you have out Sunday morning?" To worsen matters, attendances were compared not only numberwise, but percentagewise, offeringwise, visitorwise, and musicwise. Pride pressures a pastor to come out on top.

To gain victory in this area the pastor needs to meditate on Him Who came not to be chief, but to be a servant.

Other dangers exist, like desire for power, fear of failure, discouragement, and gluttony (rarely mentioned), but these are certainly some of the perils to which the clergy have always been susceptible.

THE DEMANDING ATTITUDE OF CHURCH BOARDS

In addition to these pitfalls is a growing trend of church boards to come down hard on their pastors. Like businessmen, church officials tend to look at the bottom line. If attendances and offerings are not growing, the pastor's job is in jeopardy. It's the old strategy, "If the team is losing, fire the coach."

Seemingly, congregations are dismissing pastors in unprecedented numbers today. In the book, *Forced Termination*, dealing with the problems of ministers fired or forced to resign, Brooks R. Faulkner says, "It is happening among Baptists, Methodists, Presbyterians, Episcopalians, Church of the Brethren, Christian churches, and every denomination in the United States—and even the world. Some have called it an 'epidemic.'"

Associated Press religion columnist George W. Cornell in his syndicated column (2/17/90) stated, "Each year, hundreds of Baptist pastors are being summarily fired by disgruntled congregations. And such terminations are becoming an increasingly painful problem in the big Southern Baptist Convention. . . . A 1988 study found that more than 2,100 pastors were fired during an 18-month period. That means 116 ministers were fired each month, a 31% increase over the rate found in a 1984 study." Most ousted pastors had full seminary training, and in their seminary idealism could not possibly have conceived that parish life would be so rough and tumble. But they discovered that politics in the church wouldn't differ too much from politics in the courthouse. Sadly, only half the ousted pastors eventually found other pulpits, which meant the other half went into other kinds of work (*Boca Raton Sun-Sentinel*).

One stunned minister told me that he had been dismissed without advance warning for giving an altar call, having a missionary speak in the morning service, and using too many illustrations. Another minister realized some people in the church definitely wanted him to leave when they poisoned his daughter's horse!

Why are ministers dismissed at such high frequency? Many factors are involved. Some may receive a minimum of feedback, making them oblivious to the true state of affairs. An oversupply of ministers makes a church independent in its attitude. Some churches receive over a hundred résumés when their pulpits are vacant. The frenzied pace and pressures of living often spill over into church activities, creating crises. Congregations sometimes expect too much from their pastor who cannot begin to compare with the talented TV celebrity-evangelist who comes across so smoothly in the living rooms of that pastor's parishioners. Then there is the lower level of respect given pastors in general today, a behavior trait which runs counter to the biblical imperative repeated three times in the last chapter of Hebrews. There we are told to honor those in authority in the church (13:7, 17).

Dr. Tim Blanchard, former General Director of the Conservative Baptist Association of America, reflected in the 1989 winter issue of *Conservative Baptist* on a collage of church situations he had seen during the two previous years. "Pastors have been compared unfavorably to Chuck Swindoll and John MacArthur in preaching, required to be away from their families almost every night, fired while on vacation, forced to live in parsonages unfit by any normal standards, undercut and lied about by carnally opinionated leaders, criticized openly in group meetings, and more. These are ministry conditions which, over time, would cause physical and emotional problems for most people."

Admittedly, sometimes pastors bring about their own downfall, even defrocking, through their own stupidity, rigidity, incompetence, immorality and betrayal of confidence. Also, on the other hand, some neurotic trouble-maker or intransigent church clique may make it impossible for a worthy pastor to remain in the church.

But despite these cases on both extremes in which pastors have either merited their dismissal, or have been ruthlessly terminated, large numbers are fired simply because the bottom line indicates no numerical growth in attendance or offerings. A word should be offered in defense of the small church. Church growth experts tell us that approximately one-half of all the congregations in American Protestantism average fewer than 75 at the principal weekly worship service. About 200,000 Protestant congregations have fewer than 100 at their main worship service. Three-quarters of our churches have fewer than 150. Only 5 percent average higher than 350. Lincoln said, "God must have loved the common man—He made so many of them." Perhaps it could also be said, "God loves the little church—He made so many of them."

"Small is beautiful" may be true of small churches, for often people wish to identify with a caring fellowship and not get swallowed up in a huge congregation. Though large churches may organize care circles to meet individual needs, often a small neighborhood church can meet needs which a larger ministry fails to do. Also, sometimes unfortunately, small churches permit folks who crave preeminence to be big fish in a small pond.

Admittedly, larger churches have the resources like auditoriums and money to bring in celebrity speakers and singers, and to promote major seminars. (I'll never forget what Corrie ten Boom said to me in all humility after a service in our church which registered our largest attendance ever—over a thousand, "I never go to a church this small!")

We should not forget that certain conditions prevail which make it impossible for certain churches to grow, whoever their pastor. Also, bottom-line attendances and offerings are not the only criteria to measure success. How about spiritual growth in parishioners' lives? As D. L. Moody put it, "Converts should be weighed as well as counted."

THE VOCATIONAL STRESS OF THE PASTORATE

Because of occupational stress, it's tough to be a minister today. No matter who we are or what we do, some stress is unavoidable. Life is not a bed of roses without thorns, nor a sea of smooth sailing without storms. And some stress is good, helping us mature. However, stress seems to attack us in unparalleled volume today. Stress has been called America's "public enemy number one" and "the affliction of the twentieth century" (Joel Wells, *Coping in the Eighties*, 95, 96).

Clergymen have not escaped this scourge. A denominational executive recently told me that ministers, and even entire denominations, once considered excellent risks, are now finding it increasingly difficult to obtain health policies, because so many have become ill under the pressures of the ministry.

An article, "The Vocational Stress of Ministry," cites three built-in factors that fuel stress (Dr. Michael G. McBride, *Ministry*. January 1989, 4-7).

The Minister's Multiplicity of Roles

Today's minister must perform several roles. In his chapter, "The Protestant Parish Minister's Integrating Roles," Samuel Blizzard identifies fourteen categories. Five of these roles are traditional: believer-saint, scholar, evangelist, liturgist, and father-shepherd. Eight have a contemporary orientation: the interpersonal relations specialist, the parish promoter, the community problem solver, the educator, the specialist in a sub-culture, the representative of the church-at-large, the lay minister, and the church politician (*The Minister's Own Mental Health*, 145,146).

David Lloyd George, former Prime Minister of Great Britain and eloquent political speaker, was conversing with Dr. James Black, then a pastor in Edinburgh, on the theme of preaching. The gifted Welshman said, "I don't know how you ministers do it. . . . I don't need to create my own atmosphere; it is there before me, electric and buoyant; my audience cheers the tritest remark or the most inane joke. But you are in the same place, speaking to the same people, twice a Sunday. The people don't come expecting fireworks or to be amused. And you have to speak, by and large, always on the same subject, and you have to stir or create your own atmosphere. I think that to be a minister in a settled church is one of the hardest arts of speaking known to me" (David MacLennan, *Resources for Sermon Preparation*, 7).

And preaching is just one of the multitudinous duties which keep a minister rushing around at the speed of sound to try to beat the clock. How well I recall one Friday evening when I was anticipating a 7:30 P.M. wedding rehearsal at the church nearly two blocks away. At 7 P.M. word came of an elderly man struck dead by a car two blocks up the street the other way from the church. His body was still on the road when I arrived. I sent word to the church that I would be delayed and spent the next hour visiting in three homes of loved ones, all close by. Then I walked to the church and conducted the rehearsal, shifting gears from my role as a comforter to one of joyful supervisor.

The Minister's Vulnerability to Various Role Expectations

Within the congregation are diverse groups with varying expectations, like teenagers and senior citizens. The pastor stands in the cross-fire of opposites, between fanatics and the lukewarm, between rich and poor, between avant-garde and conservatives with the motto, "We've never done it this way before." Often he has to mediate between the denominationally imposed program and his congregation's values. And he may have to contend with a hidden church boss or a powerful clique.

If a pastor has to spend a large portion of his time and energy in oiling the organizational machinery, his inability to lead his church into meaningful community outreach will prove disillusioning. Someone likened such a pastor to a coach who never leads his team into a real game because he spends so much time just getting his players to play together.

The Minister's High Visibility

Not only must a pastor possess a wide range of skills, but he must perform his roles in a high visibility setting. Under constant observation, he lives in a fishbowl. His family may experience no privacy. To enjoy days off they may have to leave home. In many churches the minister's salary is printed in the annual budget, and even voted on in a public meeting.

A church bulletin carried this description of the perfect preacher. "He works from 8 A.M. to 10 P.M. in every type of work from preaching to custodial services. He makes $60 a week (more today), wears good clothes, buys good books regularly, has a nice family, drives a good car, and gives $30 a week to the church. He is 26 years old and has been preaching for 30 years. He is tall and short, thin and heavy set, handsome. He has one brown eye and one blue, hair parted in the middle, left side dark and straight, the right brown and wavy. He has a burning desire to work with teenagers and spends all his time with older folks. He smiles all the time with a straight face because he has a sense of humor that keeps him seriously dedicated to his work. He makes 15 calls a day on church members, spends all his time evangelizing the unchurched, and is never out of his office" (Grace U.M. Church, Newsletter, Davenport, Iowa).

Consequences of Ministerial Stress

A multiplicity of duties, role expectation, and high visibility may bring on tension and anxiety which result in confusion, loss of self-esteem, psychosomatic illness leading to or speeding up existing organic disease, indecision, depression, and even immobilization. It's something like the little dog, Skip, that died mysteriously. The vet finally figured it out. The family parrot could say only two sentences, "Come here, Skip," and "Skip, go back and lie down." The parrot would order Skip to come, and Skip would come. No sooner would Skip come than the parrot would immediately order the dog to go back. The parrot kept repeating the two commands one after another till the dog fell dead from exhaustion.

A final consequence of role strain is sexual attraction and involvement. In his above-mentioned article Dr. McBride reports an experiment that demonstrates this effect. Two bridges span the Capilano River in British Columbia, Canada, one a narrow, wobbly suspension bridge swinging 30 feet above the rocky canyon, the other a solid bridge only 10 feet above a calm brook. Admittedly, walking the high bridge causes more tension. The experimenting psychologists had an attractive female approach male subjects as they walked across the bridges. This female asked the men to complete a short questionnaire showing some pictures of people. Also, she gave each man her phone number in case he wanted to know the results of the study. The psychologists predicted that the men who were on the high bridge would be more physiologically aroused than those on the low bridge, and that they would interpret this arousal as interpersonal and sexual attraction to the female experimenter.

The responses confirmed these predictions in two ways. First, the men on the high bridge tended to see sexual themes in the pictures. More significant, 50 percent of the men on the high bridge phoned the female, whereas only 12 percent of those on the low bridge did so. Dr. McBride draws this conclusion from his experiment. The role strains of pastors who deal frequently with female church members may lead to tension and anxiety, which, in turn, create a state of physiological arousal which in the company of certain women may be interpreted as sexual attraction.

TODAY'S CULTURE SEEMS TO MAKE PASTORING TOUGHER THAN EVER

Though every generation has probably thought it lived in the roughest of times, today's seminary graduate faces a world far different from the world his pastor entered a generation ago. For example, family values have degenerated. Couples living together unmarried, divorce, and little discipline in the home make for instability. As a pastor I noticed that the new New York state marriage license issued a few years ago has space on which to list several previous marriages, whereas the previous license had room for just one previous marriage.

An official of a prestigious college told me that the school now requires all students to list in order of preference the persons to be notified in case of emergency. A large number of students, he said, have an imposing hierarchy of stepmothers, stepfathers, and half sisters and half brothers, in addition to their own parents and full siblings.

People talk openly on matters never discussed in public before. TV is becoming increasingly sexually explicit. X-rated videos are available to youth at most every street corner. Homosexuals blatantly announce their preference. Believers are materialistic and endlessly busy in the pursuit of an affluent lifestyle, if not just plain survival. Our pluralistic society makes it tough to proclaim Christ as the only way without hearing ourselves called bigots.

Business responsibilities and pleasure jaunts have almost finished the Sunday evening service. Someone, noting the radical change in Sunday observance, remarked, "Our great, great grandfathers called it the holy sabbath; our great grandfathers, the sabbath; our grandfathers, the Lord's Day; our fathers, Sunday; but our children call it the weekend, and many think it's getting weaker all the time." To get people back to church after the summer is becoming increasingly difficult. Because people take off so many weekends, it's hard to find dedicated, consistent Sunday school teachers, youth leaders, choir members and other church workers. Ethical issues confront us: abortion, test-tube babies, genetic engineering, euthanasia, the homeless, pacifism, apartheid, and capital punishment, to name a few. Parishioners who are almost as well-informed on these topics look for an answer from their pastors, calling on them to defend their oft-repeated claim that the Bible has the solution to all our problems.

Of course, some good trends have shown up like the interest in defining, discovering and developing one's spiritual gifts, the presence of thousands of small groups meeting in homes for Bible study, prayer and fellowship, flexibility in worship forms, and a swing away from the fishbowl mentality, thus permitting the pastor's family more freedom and independence.

Dr. Joseph M. Stowell, president of Moody Bible Institute, wrote in *Moody Alumni* (Winter 1988-9, p. 2), "Quite frankly, I think that pastoring today is tougher than it's ever been before. People are more distracted, less committed. The competition of stellar superstars piped directly into our homes through radio and cassette, and the phenomenal impact of a secular, paganized media has all made the terrain on the pastor's path rather tough. Our pastors find themselves struggling with their place, their people, their power. Pocketbook issues often keep them free of self-sufficiency." Note the description of church people today, so aptly summed up in those two phrases, "More distracted, less committed."

THE NEED FOR LONGER PASTORATES

Strange as it may seem, at one time in American history pastors ministered to the same church their entire professional lifetime. A study of Yale College graduates from 1702 to 1775 reveals that 79 percent of those who became pastors served one congregation or parish all their lives. Only 7 percent had more than two charges. Termed "transient" pastors, this small group were deemed "ne'er do wells," because they failed to fashion a continuing relationship with one congregation. This "one church" practice reflected the culture of that era when most people lived out their lives in one place.

How different from today when the average length of a pastorate seems to be around three to four years. Lyle E. Schaller, church administration expert, tells us over and over again in his books that, while there are many exceptions to this generalization, from the congregation's perspective the most effective years of a pastorate rarely begin before the fourth or fifth or sixth, or seventh, and sometimes even the eighth, year of that pastorate (e.g., *Survival Tactics in the Parish*, 27) The minister who moves on after two or three years may be robbing his congregation of a potentially productive ministry in that place.

Though a long pastorate is no guarantee of church growth, congregations do not usually enjoy sustained rapid growth without the benefit of a long pastorate. Thus, if a pastor wants to have an effective ministry in a church, he must be able to survive the tribulations long enough to build a strong foundation of meaningful relationships on which to expand and reach out.

Lyle E. Schaller, in the same book, suggests "three of the essential characteristics for survival in the parish ministry: getting plenty of sleep every day, a clear sense of self-identity, and a remarkable ability to ignore trifling diversions" (13). In this volume I will add to these essentials, illustrating from my parish experience the techniques that helped me survive forty years in the same church.

Times may be tough, but a door of opportunity stands wide open for pastors to endure hardness like good soldiers of Jesus Christ.

2

Be Sure of Your Call

Two young men asked to see me in my study. Splendid fellows, just graduating from college, they were pondering career choices. Both had been active in our youth groups while growing up, and they were involved in Christian witness away at college. Theirs was a question faced by most ministerial candidates.

"Pastor, how does a person tell if he should become a pastor?"

I gave them the same answer I had given the approximately dozen young men from our congregation who through the years have entered the pastorate. Naturally, we chatted about the subject for a little while, but my answer in capsule was simply, "If you can stay out of the ministry, stay out. But if you must say with the apostle Paul, 'Woe is unto me, if I preach not the gospel!' (1 Cor. 9:16), then make plans to become a pastor."

Today one of the boys is a successful businessman and active in Christian work, having served as Sunday school superintendent and youth advisor. He could not say, "Woe is me, if I preach not." The other has since graduated from seminary and for six years has pastored a thriving Long Island church. He could not shake his burden for the pastorate.

This incident reminded me of a similar interview over 40 years before, when my 24-year-old friend and I, just 16, both active in Christian activity, asked our pastor the same question in his office in Hamilton, Ontario, Canada. He gave us the same answer, "If you can stay out, stay out. Only enter the ministry if you can say with the apostle Paul, 'Woe is unto me, if I preach not the gospel!'" My friend could stay out, had a successful business career, and never forgot to use his business ability in serving the local church. I could not stay out, so after ministerial schooling, I spent 45 years in the pastorate.

The ministry today can be tough and rough. To survive, a pastor needs to know that God has called him. Otherwise, the task may be overwhelming. But how can we know the call of God?

AN INTENSE DESIRE FOR THE MINISTRY

During a state governor's election campaign someone asked a candidate, "Why seek office when political life is so trying?" Came the reply, "You have to have the fire in your bones."

The ministry is not for those who cannot make a success in any other line of work. Rather, there must be a deep burden for the work. C. H. Spurgeon said for "a true call to the ministry there must be an irresistible, overwhelming craving and raging thirst for telling to others what God has done to our own souls" (*Lectures to My Students*, 23).

Spurgeon warned his class of ministerial students, "If any student in this room could be content to be a newspaper editor, or a grocer, or a farmer, or a doctor, or a lawyer, or a senator, or a king, in the name of heaven and earth let him go his way; he is not the man in whom dwells the Spirit of God in its fullness, for a man so filled with God would utterly weary of any pursuit but that for which his inmost soul pants. If, on the other hand, you can say that for all the wealth of both the Indies you could not and dare not espouse any other calling so as to be put aside from preaching the gospel of Jesus Christ, then, depend upon it, if other things be equally satisfactory, you have the signs of this apostleship. We must feel that woe is unto us if we preach not the gospel; the Word of God must be unto us as fire in our bones, otherwise, if we undertake the ministry, we shall be unhappy in it, shall be unable to bear the self-denials incident to it, and shall be of little service to those among whom we minister. I speak of self-denials, and well I may; for the true pastor's work is full of them, and without a love to his calling he will soon succumb, and either leave the drudgery, or move on in discontent, burdened with a monotony as tiresome as that of a blind horse in a mill" (23, 24).

In an interview after Lausanne Conference II in 1989 John Stott, rector emeritus of All Souls Church in London, said regarding his decision to enter the ministry, "I loved Cambridge, and felt attracted to the academic life, but God called me to the pastorate" (*Christianity Today*, 8 September 1989, 63).

This strong inclination for the ministry must not be some momentary impulse or temporary fascination with outward honors that might accompany the position of a pastor. Rather, it must be the outgrowth of reverent consideration and earnest prayer. Mere infatuation with the possibility of pastoral service will fade. A true call will persist when other offers try to turn us aside, and will be a bulwark for survival when the going gets tough.

The Gifts to Equip for the Pastorate

The strong desire to become a pastor must be accompanied by the gifts necessary for that office, including an aptness to teach, and a degree of speaking ability. A person need not display oratorical prowess the first time he preaches, for some of the noblest pulpiteers were not fluent in their early attempts. But if some aptitude does not soon show itself, it will not likely ever develop. He must be given a fair trial to discover whether or not he possesses this necessary gift.

A young ministerial student, home for Christmas during his second year in seminary, asked if he could give a short talk at a Sunday evening service. His material and delivery were pathetic. The next Christmas he again asked for the same privilege. Graciously wishing to give the young man every opportunity to succeed, the pastor opened the pulpit to him again. Again he flopped. As the end of his seminary training neared, the pastor wrote the school about the young man's progress. When the school replied that he had no evident gifts for preaching, nor had made any improvement after three years of schooling, the pastor did not invite him to preach any more, and later informed him that in his opinion he did not possess the call to the ministry.

To succeed in the ministry a person must possess the gifts for that calling. To that extent preachers are born, not made.

Opportunities to Minister

In the logic of things, a strong desire for the ministry may well point up the existence of the pastoral gift, which in turn suggests that an outlet will be provided for the exercise of that gift. To state it another way, a gift will be preceded by desire, and followed by opportunity to use it. In His good time the Lord will open up a ministry for His ordained and gifted servants. A youthful aspirant should be willing to begin with menial tasks in the Lord's vineyard. Faithfulness in little things will prepare one for openings of larger service later.

My Personal Call to the Ministry

It seems hard to realize it now, but for me to speak in public in my early teen years was a near impossibility. Oral composition was my poorest subject in high school. To give a speech in class, as required three or four times each year, was a terrifying experience. To be up front before any crowd almost paralyzed me with stage fright. At the time I was not a Christian, and the ministry was farthest from my mind.

At fifteen years of age I became a believer. Up to this time church, which my godly parents made me attend Sunday morning and evening, had been a bore; now I liked to go. Previously, I read trashy literature; now I became interested in Christian books. Before, I never went to our youth meeting; now I never missed. Remarkably, I began to have a desire to communicate my faith, not only privately, but in public settings.

A former Sunday school teacher took me under his wing, and nurtured me along. When he became pastor of a nearby church, I expressed an interest in teaching Sunday school. Immediately he encouraged me, showing me how to organize a lesson. Four days past my sixeenth birthday, I began teaching a class and taught it regularly for two years till I left for ministerial training.

Our church in Hamilton, Ontario, Canada, had a thriving youth work with two groups, one with 100 in attendance every week, the other with 50. At sixteen I was eligible for membership, providentially choosing the smaller group, not knowing that often I would be asked to participate by giving a short talk. I recall using the material in a quarterly to write out a ten-minute message, memorizing it, rehearsing it many times in front of a mirror, then somehow stifling my stage fright, to give a well-received talk. This became a monthly ritual.

Then I began to receive invitations to speak in other youth groups, in our church's summer center-city open-air meetings, in rescue missions, and in good-sized young men's Sunday school classes. How well I remember the owner of a downtown Christian bookstore, and leader of an open Brethren assembly, inviting me to give the message one Sunday evening. At the end, he kindly advised me that my message didn't quite fit. I had spoken on reasons why people should accept Christ in their teenage years— to a congregation all in mid or late life! Then he invited me back the next month, anticipating a more appropriate message.

As I write, I'm looking at a faded piece of notepaper on which I had typed a list of all my speaking engagements for the two years between high school and ministerial school, when I was 17 and 18. (One year was spent in completing a business college course, and the other working in an office.) As I look at this list, I see entries on an average of one a week during this period. These frequent opportunities to speak confirmed for this teenager, whose worst high school subject had been oral composition, a growing conviction that the Lord was calling him into the ministry. It was about this time that my friend and I made an appointment to ask our pastor, as recorded at the beginning of this chapter, how a person could tell whether or not he should enter the ministry.

DEVELOPMENT OF THE PASTORAL GIFT

Since we are not ornaments, but instruments, our gifts should be cultivated. The desire for the pastoral gift should lead to its discovery and deployment. However, along the way it may need to be polished. Today, pastors require training. At one time the minister was the best educated person in the community. That day has long since passed. Many laymen today, already college graduates and well informed, are developing their spiritual gifts in formal study correspondence courses, adult Bible studies, or in evening Bible school. How much more does a pastor need to sharpen his call by college and seminary study. God, the Author of all truth, places no premium on ignorance.

My pastor strongly recommended Bible school, so I went first to Moody Bible Institute in Chicago where I graduated from the Pastors Course. Then followed Wheaton College. After that, Eastern Baptist Seminary in Philadelphia. A year after seminary, in my first pastorate, I received an M.A. in Philosophy from the University of Pennsylvania.

During my schooling various events served to confirm my calling to the ministry. In my final year at Moody I was selected by the Practical Work Director to fill preaching engagements. Also, I was voted by the men of my class to represent them as speaker at graduation. This meant several private speech-coaching sessions prior to commencement.

Before my senior year at Wheaton, I was invited to be summer assistant at my home church in Hamilton, Canada. Because the pastor was gone for six weeks, it meant speaking live on the radio six mornings a week, leading the Sunday services and speaking one of the Sundays, hospital and shut-in visitation, conducting a funeral, running the open-air meetings, and giving a message at several other church youth groups. Altogether, I counted 68 speaking engagements that July and August.

Then in my senior year at Wheaton I entered the college's annual oratorical contest, finishing second in the men's division. Chosen to represent Wheaton in state oratory, I finished fourth in a contest of ten Illinois colleges. To prepare for the competition I received hours of free coaching from a couple of speech professors. One thing they corrected was my yelling in the delivery of my speech. My pastor had been the ranting and raving type, and I had imitated his style. They toned me down, for college oratory does not look kindly on such bombastics. I followed their advice. Didn't that student, whose worst high school subject had been oral composition, need all possible help?

That wasn't all the speech coaching I received. At that annual Wheaton college oratorical contest I met Bernice, the girl who was to become my wife. A freshman, she won the girl's division. Later, in married life, a graduate with a speech major, she wanted to critique my sermon late Sunday nights. After some helpful evaluations, I suggested that she wait till Monday morning, and by then, like all my parishioners, she had forgotten what the sermon was about! But through the years she has given me constructive criticism.

The summer immediately after graduation from Wheaton I traveled with the Wheaton College Quintet, officially authorized to represent the school. I joined a quartet of talented singers as the speaker, holding about 88 meetings all the way from Duluth, Minnesota, to San Diego, California, to New Castle, Pennsylvania—invaluable training for a ministerial aspirant.

Delight in the Pastorate

When a person finally finds himself as pastor of a church, he may well exclaim, "I've found it! This is it!" Later on he may enthusiastically affirm, "This is what I'd rather be doing than anything else in the world. I so enjoy it! This is my thing. This turns me on!" He bubbles over when he talks of the ministry, despite all its difficulties.

How wrong to assume that, because we enjoy pastoring, we cannot be in God's will. Or, on the contrary, to deduce that because something is distasteful, it must be God's plan for us. Wouldn't the Lord more likely assign us a ministry which brings pleasure, not misery? Like Jesus, in doing the Father's will, we should find delight, not drudgery. Great satisfaction, settling dove-like over our hearts, confirms that God has placed us in the pastorate for such a time as this.

For many ministers the pastorate is the highest calling possible, envied by angels who would love to proclaim the gospel. Pastors should remind themselves regularly of their high and holy privilege. They should never lose their sense of wonder over the fact that the Lord chose them to be shepherds of His flock. An appropriate sense of calling will not only enable a pastor to better survive but also to accomplish much more.

In my case, I can truthfully say that the ministry has been a delight. At my retirement dinner in 1989 I made this statement, "These 40 years have been the happiest years of my life. I came here at 30, and now I'm the proverbial three score years and ten. For 40 years I have breathed, slept, ate, dreamed and lived this church. The time has sped by so quickly. They have been blessed, wonderful years—and I have only the most wonderful of memories."

CONFIRMATION OF THE CALL BY FELLOW-BELIEVERS

A person should submit his claim of call to the scrutiny of loving and discerning brothers. The crowning confirmation that he does possess the pastoral gift is recognition by others. The ministry, thus, is not the result of one call, but of two: the minister's and the church's. The candidate cannot make up his mind in isolation, but he must find some support from the people among whom he ministers, often his home church.

Historians tell us that in Reformation times the call of the church came first. When others detected the pastoral gift in some young person, they would urge him to stir up that gift. Then, if he sensed the inner call, he would move forward with the support of everyone. In any case, the candidate's call required a demonstration of talents approved by the church as evidence of that call.

Considerable weight must be attached to the estimate of godly men and women. In by far the majority of cases, their prayerful opinion will be an accurate one. This is why prospective seminary students are usually required to secure the endorsement of their home church. A license to preach is recognition by a local fellowship of the candidate's suitability for the ministry. Sometimes a local group will put their stamp of approval on a young man, who, though lacking some of their suggested standards for ordination, demonstrates beyond any shadow of doubt that on him rests the stamp of divine ordination.

Sometimes earthly fellowships may fail at first to recognize gifted men. G. Campbell Morgan was rejected for the ministry at age 25. His father wired him, "Rejected on earth, accepted in heaven." Despite that rejection, in the next 25 years Dr. Morgan won worldwide recognition as pastor, author, college president, and Bible teacher.

John Newton, author of "Amazing Grace," was finally ordained just before his fortieth birthday by the Church of England only after painstaking preparation and two rejections for ordination.

It should be emphasized that the pastoral office requires far more than the ability to speak in public. Says Spurgeon, "There must be other talents to complete the pastoral character. Sound judgment and solid experience must instruct you; gentle manners and loving affections must sway you; firmness and courage must be manifest; and tenderness and sympathy must not be lacking. Gifts administrative in ruling well will be as requisite as gifts instructive in teaching well. You must be fitted to lead, prepared to endure, and able to persevere. In grace, you should be head and shoulders above the rest of the people, able to be their father and counselor. Read carefully the qualifications of a bishop given in 1 Tim. 3:2-7, and in Titus 1:6-9" (*Lectures to My Students*, 28).

SOME MEASURE OF SUCCESS

Unless a pastor sees some measure of conversions and growth in grace in the congregation, he may conclude he has made a mistake. Results will vary in different churches, for some situations are tougher than others, but some results are necessary as a seal of approval. To pastor a church, and see nothing happen year in and year out, can raise doubt as to the authenticity of one's vocation.

A preacher may work wonders in one location, serving many years, seeing numerical and spiritual growth, then move to another location, or even return to his original church years later, and not be able to duplicate his earlier success. I knew a preacher from the north who, after three decades of solid growth, new buildings, and big budgets, moved south and became pastor of a struggling church, ripped by internal problems. After a short while, he resigned, unable to make a go of it. Same pastor— success in one place, but not in the other.

I think of my home church in Hamilton, Canada, started around the turn of the century by a handful of people, meeting in a hall Sunday evenings, led by a converted blacksmith, Peter W. Philpott. The growing crowds required the renting of a downtown theater. Finally a church edifice was built, seating 1,000. My parents, who were won to Christ through Philpott's preaching, told me that to get a seat on a Sunday night required arrival an hour ahead of time. The church continued to thrive with overflow P.M. services for years, till Philpott accepted a call to Moody Church, Chicago, in 1922. After another pastorate, at the Church of the Open door in Los Angeles, Philpott returned to Hamilton in 1936 as interim pastor for one year. But at this time he could not fill the church. Only fourteen years earlier the building overflowed with people; now the building was only partly full. Same pastor, same church, but not the same results.

Perhaps there's a lesson here. When a church blossoms, the credit may not totally belong to the pastor, for there may be other contributing factors. Contrariwise, when a church fades, the blame likely does not rest fully on the pastor either, for other factors probably enter in. What we call success is relative, but if one has been called to the ministry, faithfulness is what the Lord requires. In the day of His evaluation, many who were first down here will be last up there, and many who were last down here will be first up there.

SENSE OF GOD'S CALL THROUGHOUT ONE'S MINISTRY

When I announced my retirement in 1989, I said, "With all my heart I believe it was God's will for me to come to this church forty years ago. I never doubted that God guided my coming here." Then I went on to say, "With all my heart I believe it was the will of God for me to stay here all these years. Through the years I have received a thick sheaf of letters, as well as numerous phone calls, from search committees of churches looking for a pastor. I would answer these letters immediately, and always the same way, stating that I was convinced that God's will for me was to remain in Nanuet. My wife would ask, 'Why don't you pray about these invitations?' My answer was always, 'There's no need to pray about anything when you are certain of God's call.' I was convinced then, and still am, that it was God's will for me to be here these four decades."

Then I concluded, "And now, I am just as convinced that it is in the Lord's will for me to step aside at this time, relinquish this pastorate, and retire. Not a shadow of doubt exists in my mind." (Four people wept and 400 cheered!!!) And since resigning, I can say with all my heart that now the Lord's will for me is retirement. Pressures are off, and I have enough speaking engagements and writing assignments to keep me as busy as I wish to be.

Probably most believers can recall a time or two when along the Christian path the Lord confirmed His care for them in some special way. One such occasion stands out in my memory. The year was 1972. On a Monday morning I flew to Hamilton, Canada, where my father had just undergone major surgery. I was due back in New York late in the week to tape radio programs. Monday night, after visiting my father in the hospital, my mother served dessert to some close family friends. Tuesday morning I found my mother on the kitchen floor, victim of a stroke. Thursday, on doctor's orders I called for the ambulance to take her to the hospital. That meant I would be leaving my parents, both in their ninetieth year, in the same hospital, until I could return the following Monday. I was bewildered. I needed advice, but where could I turn?

At noontime the day before flying back to New York, I decided to walk downtown. Stepping into a department store, I noticed a big crowd shopping on sale day. About to leave, I saw a man a few yards away smiling in my direction. Thinking the smile was meant for someone else, I edged toward the door, but observed that he kept smiling and moving toward me. Reaching me, he asked, "Aren't you Les Flynn?" When I answered yes, he said, "My name is Alan Marshall."

His name rang a bell. Often my parents had spoken of a lawyer in their church of unimpeachable character and top ability. In fact, they had not only suggested verbally to me to seek his counsel if anything should ever happen to them, but also had written his name in a note, which I later found attached to their will as the lawyer to contact. So I exclaimed, "I know who you are. You're a lawyer. You attend my parents' church!" Then mentioning my parents' hospitalization, I said, "I'm going to need your help!"

My parents both passed away within the next six weeks. Alan Marshall took care of their legal affairs quickly and efficiently. Though I had never met him, he recognized me in the store that noon because he had heard me preach on several occasions in my parents' church. Later he told me something startling and significant. He said he never frequented that particular department store. He did not know why on his noon hour that particular day he wandered in.

But I know why he entered that store. I needed help that day. So, the Lord led a man into a busy store to spot me midst a crowd of shoppers, 500 miles from home, recognize me and introduce himself. It was as if the Lord was saying to me, "Child of Mine, I know you're in trouble. I know you need help. And I have sent it to you." To me, it was a confirmation, not only of God's love and sovereignty, but also of His continuing call to me as a minister of Jesus Christ.

3

Put Others to Work

One summer morning in the early '80s the mail brought an unusual request. A letter from Denver Seminary asked me to do a 12-minute video on my philosophy of church leadership. They planned to use it as part of their faculty retreat program. If I were agreeable, they would mail me a blank video.

In reply, I suggested that they would not be interested in my method of church management, giving the following reasons. I had not been to a meeting of my Board of Trustees for 30 years. Nor did I attend meetings of the Missionary Committee, leaving decisions on missionary matters to their wisdom. Nor did I join with the Nominating Committee when they selected the slate of church officers for the next year. Also, whenever we needed a new minister of youth, I left the recommendation completely in the hands of a search committee. I added that I did not meet the current youth minister till he was already on the job.

To my surprise, the seminary answered that a recital of this "hands off" model of leadership was exactly what they were looking for. So, I did the video. Of course, they secured videos of other types of pastoral leadership as well.

Administrative analysts single out three major modes of church leadership: the *dictatorial*, where the pastor rules with an iron hand; the *consultative*, where the pastor, though making the decisions, uses the skills and input of others in plan-formulating; and the *participative*, where the pastor, while remaining the team leader, regards team members as equals and their input welcome, even when disagreeing with him. My type of church leadership definitely fell in this third category. I am a firm believer in sharing the work, the decisions and the responsibility in church life. Putting others to work has been for me a vital key to sanity and survival in the ministry.

THE DUTIES OF THE MINISTRY ARE OVERWHELMING

Today's minister is expected to be a jack-of-all-trades: scholar, financier, visitor, public relations expert, organizer, administrator, preacher, teacher, typist, counselor, social worker, file clerk, correspondent, journalist, educator, real estate agent, shepherd, evangelist, program director, prophet, worship leader, chief executive officer, computer operator, director of the duplicator, and let's not forget theologian too.

Every Saturday night pastors feel frustrated because another week has rolled around before the list of items needing to be done could be checked off. Most pastors carry a work load heavier than they can efficiently handle. One said, "I could work day and night for weeks and not get done all the things I'm supposed to do." Another sighed that he would be far better off if Sunday came around only once every two weeks.

Few occupations demand so many hours per week of work as does the ministry. Surveys show that many business executives work from 50 to 60 hours a week. A poll of clergymen revealed that many work 70 hours a week.

Members of a congregation were asked to indicate on a questionnaire how many hours they felt their pastor should devote per week to each of the following tasks: preparing sermons, personal interviews, administering the affairs of the church, committee meetings, budget planning and promotion, community activities, youth groups, comforting the bereaved, and marriage counseling. Totals on the answers averaged 82 hours per week. One member proposed 200 hours. (A week has only 168 hours!)

Feverish activity to assume all obligations with some degree of effectiveness has been listed as one cause of ministerial breakdown. The exhausting marathon of endless, diverse duties, performed against the squeeze of dwindling time, damages like a car traveling with the emergency brake on, or frustrates like racing the engine with the car in neutral—plenty of noise but no progress. The strain will inevitably show up as in one nervous executive who, asking his secretary where his pencil was and told it was behind his ear, snapped, "I'm a busy man. Which ear?"

Most pastors do not wish to avoid work, but would like to work more efficiently. The solution is not found in any magical, push-button formula. But hard work harnessed to simple, time-saving methods will enable ministers to stay on top of their work instead of sinking beneath the load. These time-saving techniques, found in a typical time-management manual (e.g., respecting the worth of time, planning ahead, making a schedule, efficient layout of the work area, starting earlier, using spare minutes, doing it now), will rid a pastor of many irritations, pressures, frustrations, and the nagging anxiety of unfinished jobs. But one of the most fruitful policies to help a pastor "work smarter, not harder," is to put others to work.

DELEGATING IS A BIBLICAL PRINCIPLE

Years ago, when our church purchased a mimeograph machine, the salesman offered to teach me how to operate it. Politely I showed him the door. I have never mimeographed a line in my life. I do not know how, and refuse to learn. My refusal to mimeograph does not stem from any aversion to soiling my hands but from dislike of devoting valuable time to tasks which can be done by volunteer or staff secretaries. Later I did learn how to operate a new copy machine and took a short course on operating a computer, machines essential in sermon research. But I never did learn anything about them mechanically. Whenever any church apparatus broke down, the secretaries, knowing my ineptitude, either repaired it themselves, or called in outside help.

Here is my philosophy. When I have been trained to minister the Word publicly from the pulpit, and privately in counsel, why should I give precious hours to what many others can so ably do? I need every possible minute to study and nurture the souls entrusted to my care. D. L. Moody said, "Put ten men to work rather than do the work of ten men!" Assigning work to ten men multiplies a pastor's time tenfold. One pastor operated on the policy: I never do anything that someone else can do.

In refusing to learn mimeographing I was following a scriptural principle, examples of which are found in both Old and New Testaments. In the growing early church the Hellenistic element murmured against the Hebrews, claiming their widows were neglected in the daily distribution of alms. Not wishing to be diverted from their prime duties, the apostles wisely had the church elect seven gifted and godly men to take over the business of alms distribution. This freed the apostles to continue their main ministry of the Word and prayer. We read the result, "The word of God increased; and the number of the disciples multiplied in Jerusalem greatly" (Acts 6:7).

Many fine pastors have seen their influence erode as their ministries have been sidetracked to table-serving. One influential minister, recognizing that the good is the enemy of the best, took inventory of his activities, then determined to give up membership in most of his clubs—fraternal, civic, and social—which had been subtly sapping away dozens of hours. The hours then released for vital areas of his vocation yielded considerable growth in his church, both numerical and spiritual.

In an Old Testament story, Jethro, visiting Moses in the wilderness, noticed that his son-in-law was wearing himself out by acting as judge for every complaint arising among the people. Perhaps Moses had not delegated authority to anyone because he doubted the ability of his countrymen so recently removed from serfdom. To save both the time and strength of Moses, Jethro recommended the appointment of subordinate judges to handle all cases except those too difficult, which would be referred to Moses. So Moses chose capable men to rule over thousands, hundreds, fifties, and tens (Exodus 18:13-27).

Because he could not shepherd more than one church at a time, Paul arranged for elders to feed and lead the flock in every church. On their first missionary journey Paul and Barnabas had as their assistant John Mark who by performing minor errands released the apostles for their important tasks (Acts 13:5). The book of Acts depicts Paul surrounded by a team of men whom he was training and sending out to witness in places he could not visit. Luke, Demas, Crescens, Titus, Timothy, Silas, and Tychicus were among the host of helpers whose labors liberated Paul for his vast preaching and literary endeavors.

When today's pastor delegates work, he follows in the train of men like Moses, the Twelve, Paul, and also the Lord Jesus, all of whom saved time, and helped themselves survive in their ministry by putting others to work.

DECIDE WHAT IS IMPORTANT, DELEGATE THE REST

With no more hours than anyone else, but with so much to do, the pastor must select priority projects, then transfer other tasks to responsible helpers. After his heart attack President Eisenhower was forced to curtail his work load drastically. So he decided to schedule fewer appointments and social engagements, and to delegate correspondence and routine matters, limiting himself to paramount issues. Suppose every pastor had to cut his schedule in half. Would he not discover ways of getting others to relieve him of the less consequential? Asked the secret of his success, one manager replied, "I work at essentials rather than trivialities."

My wife and I stayed overnight at the home of a physician-friend who mentioned that 72 patients had passed through his office that day. When I asked how he could possibly see so many, he explained that he hadn't seen all of them personally. His nurse had handled 24 persons—all routine matters like shots or diet-data. The doctor had delegated one-third of his workload. One of the simplest ways for a pastor to conserve time is to have a good secretary to handle the run-of-the-mill details, and to weed out unimportant phone calls. I was always blessed with competent secretaries.

In a growing church it may no longer be possible for a pastor to have a direct, personal involvement with every member of his flock. The senior minister of a Texas church aptly said that with his large congregation he could no longer be a shepherd, but had to be a rancher with under-shepherds responsible for the scattered herds. Instead of spending time as before with members, he now devoted more hours to outreach.

The minister who has been the shepherd of a manageable flock, available to the cry of any hurting sheep, may find it necessary, though difficult, to delegate authority to sub-shepherds and groups, while still remaining responsive to cases of special need. One of our shepherding programs positioned members under the care of a deacon who would be available for counsel in time of need. Though the program had its defects, it freed me for the more serious crises. The pastor of a thriving church said, "I have 22 active standing committees. I put lay people to work and delegate responsibilities." So, pastors will need to put trustworthy parishioners to work.

HELP PEOPLE FIND THEIR SPIRITUAL GIFTS

Without exception every believer possesses one or more spiritual gifts. Every Christian is a gifted child of God. Pastors should help their people discover, develop and deploy their gifts in some area of ministry.

All pastors likewise possess spiritual gifts, especially those of teaching, preaching, administration and encouragement. But perhaps some pastors feel less gifted in some areas than in others. They should work within the context of their God-given strengths. A person becomes uncomfortable with himself when he is not doing what he is best suited for. So, a pastor should labor within his limits, following a coach's advice to a player, "Find out what you don't do well, then don't do it." He should exercise strong points, and get others to assist in weak areas.

I was not particularly fond of counseling. However, I was always available to those who wished to see me, but never went out of my way to encourage it. Whenever possible, I directed those seeking counsel to our associate pastor, or youth pastor. Stephen Olford, when pastor of New York City's Calvary Baptist Church, pointed out that church members themselves should assume responsibility for counseling scores of people who would then seldom need to see the minister. He cited Hebrews 10:24, 25 as teaching that it is the duty of members to encourage one another, and to see that each other is regular in church attendance.

To equip members to help each other, I set up frequent courses on counseling, taught by Christian psychiatrists, psychologists, marriage and family counselors, and personnel from a nearby Christian mental health complex. These ten-to-twelve-week courses were offered in adult Sunday school classes or weekday evening Bible institutes.

Also, I did not picture myself as possessor of unusual administrative ability. Hence, all through my ministry I refused to let my name be nominated for our denominational or para-church boards. The only exceptions began after twenty years in my pastorate when I agreed to go on two boards. Then for twenty years I served on the World Relief Commission of the National Association of Evangelicals, which required four meetings a year. I also was a trustee of Denver Conservative Baptist Seminary for fifteen years. Though this board met only twice a year, I did devote considerable administrative time and travel, serving on the Seminary's Search Committee for a new president in the '70s.

A study by the Ministers Life and Casualty Union found that 52 percent of the pastors interviewed felt that too many demands were made upon them by the administrative work of the church. To help solve this problem in my case, I followed a policy of securing competent, gifted members to take over as many administrative tasks as possible. This permitted me much more time and energy for the areas for which I was gifted, which gave me more delight, and contributed to my survival.

This is why, recalling the opening incident in this chapter, I did not attend our Trustee Board meetings for 30 years, nor the meetings of the Missionary and Nominating Committees. Nor did I ever attend Christian Education Committee meetings. However, I kept my finger on the pulse of these and all other committees through a copy of the minutes of all their meetings.

Nor did I ever lead or help in a Daily Vacation Bible School in 40 years, except to give a short talk at the final program, which happily introduced me to the parents of newcomers. But I did personally call in the home of every new member prospect within a week. As a result, almost without exception we had one or more new families come to our church each year through D.V.B.S.

Neither did I arrange the Sunday morning or evening order of worship the final 15 years of my pastorate. Our Minister of Music, son of a minister and well-versed in both Bible truth and hymnology, was more than qualified to select hymns, anthems and special numbers. With my blessing he planned the worship sequence, not necessarily following the same order every week. Recognizing his facility along this line, the church gave him the title, "Minister of Music and Worship."

I did not select the music on our weekly radio program either. With this duty assigned to capable others, I was able to concentrate on the 15-minute talk which was scripted and offered without cost to the public.

Neither did I get involved in the youth programs. That was the sphere of the Minister of Youth and the youth advisers. I did go on one retreat, put on ice skates for the first time in 20 years, and made the mistake of playing hockey with the fellows who, disregarding my ecclesiastical status, banged me around.

Another point: I did not lead our stewardship drives. Vividly I recall one financial campaign to ascertain estimated church giving for the coming year. Many hours of planning were required to make this ten-week crusade work, involving a breakfast for the more than 60 volunteers, routes and material for the many teams, plus forms for tabulations, and a host of other paper work. I remember remarking to a fellow pastor, "I had nothing to do with it, except to give two sermons on money." I recall sending a letter of commendation to our stewardship chairman for his magnificent management of the logistics of the entire campaign.

I did not lead our Senior Heirs' ministry either. A committee of senior citizens arranged the monthly menu and meetings which were presided over most entertainingly by our Associate Pastor. Likewise our couples group was handled by a couplers committee. Nor did I get involved in the operation of our bookstore.

When asked by a community group to join a committee fighting pornography, I agreed to attend several meetings. But gradually I worked in two laymen from our church who had a special interest in that battle, allowing me to withdraw to other pressing matters.

I did not become directly involved in social action protests, but I did deal with such matters on our weekly radio broadcast. I considered that my priorities and strengths pointed to the preaching of the Word, while at the same time supporting those whose convictions led them to demonstrate.

With the flow of thousands of refugees out of southeast Asia I urged the congregation to sponsor a refugee. They sponsored a young man, his wife and baby. The wife, whose physician-father had been killed in the jungle, wanted to bring over her mother and several brothers, to which the church agreed. But I kept myself free from involvement in the many details and later complications, except for one occasion when I drove the young refugee to a hospital for treatment for depression.

Some pastors seldom permit anyone else in their pulpit. But I never felt that way. Sensing that I do not possess the gift of evangelism, I periodically invited evangelists to hold crusades in our church. Realizing that other pastors and teachers possessed abilities differing from mine, I never hesitated to have Bible conferences led by gifted Bible expositors. The lone-wolf syndrome has no place in the ministry. No pastor is gifted enough, wise enough, or strong enough to live apart from others. Calling in other trained and proven teachers to minister will add considerably to the edification of a flock.

Whenever anything needed repair in the parsonage (and it was frequent), I would call on a certain trustee, who whether on or off the board, would immediately respond. We called him "Mr. Fixit." Even though plastic pipe was held up by a coat hanger, we owed him a debt of appreciation. When he moved away, other men stepped in to fill his role, for my lack of mechanical ability was well known by the congregation.

No pastor, however handy with hammer and saw, should be saddled with repairs or janitorial jobs like arranging chairs or putting out hymnals. Nor should he be bothered with minor matters like determining the frequency of piano tuning, the color of choir robes, nor the type of refreshments at the next social. Nor should he have to count the people present in the services. I had the reputation in the New York city area as "the pastor who does not know where his lighting or loud-speaking systems are."

LEARN TO SAY NO

A concert artist was asked the secret of her success. She replied, "planned neglect." She explained that when she began the study of the violin so many things demanded her attention that only after caring for such matters did she then turn to her music. With the violin getting the tail end of her time, she was getting nowhere fast. So one day she made a decision. She determined to reverse the whole procedure. In her words, "I deliberately planned to neglect everything else until my practice period was completed. That program of planned neglect accounts for my success."

A pastor needs to learn how to use the middle two letters of the alphabet: N–O. He should not become the messenger boy of every organization that wants a grace at some dinner, or a representative on some committee. Though he must not forget his responsibility to the community, he must evaluate the many demands on his time on the basis of priority. He should not be a job collector, but should follow Paul's example, "This one thing I do." He should decide the main thrust of his ministry, concentrate on that, and give up time-consuming peripheral issues.

WATCH OUT FOR CURVES!

When a pastor delegates authority, a committee may throw him a curve by making a decision which he doesn't genuinely endorse. Rather than insisting he have a voice in every decision, a pastor must learn to trust his people, and accept their action. For example, in the '60s I began a series of July and August Sunday evening programs of special music, which I called our summer festival. But I had some guidelines. The artist had to be living in or visiting our area, avoiding transportation costs, and the honorarium just $50, not an unreasonable a fee in those days. For a few years all went well. Then I turned it over to a special committee, who before long were bringing artists from afar, and paying fees up to $400. Before long, the summer music festival which annually drew fine crowds became a sizeable budget item.

I recall the installation service of a new pastor at our branch church. I had left the selection of the participants to a committee who decided to have no printed order of service, and who also failed to notify me that I was to give the installation message. Imagine my surprise when it came time for the installation sermon, to hear myself introduced as the speaker. Never did a preacher walk so slowly from the rear of a church toward a podium as I did that night, trying to give my whirling mind time to pull an appropriate sermon out of the barrel.

When you deliberately avoid serving on the Nominating Committee, you leave yourself open to working with unsuitable officers. One pastor tells of weeping for a few nights when a meek hotel doorman, whose only status was his gold braids, was elected to the church board. Suddenly the doorman became a vocal tyrant staring down at the pastor. By handling the problem with grace and patience, the pastor helped the doorman to become a spiritual dynamo. I recall a man on whom I called five years before he would join the church on profession of faith. Two years later he became chairman of property and grounds, and I had to get permission from him to borrow church chairs for a private party at the parsonage! On rare occasions folks were elected to lead, who didn't lead. Then, if I couldn't work with them, I worked around them.

On most occasions, however, officials would approach me, despite my hands-off policy, to consult on impending decisions of importance. When we put up two new buildings nine years apart, first a Sunday school addition, then a new sanctuary, I refrained from serving on the Building Committee both times. The co-contractors in charge were active members of our church, fully competent, and what did I know about putting up buildings? But when it came time for the building of the church, I did ask for two things: a pulpit up front, and a private restroom in my study. They gladly acquiesced. Also, the chairman did come privately for me to decide the specific seating capacity.

By delegating authority to a specific committee a pastor provides a measure of protection for himself, should they come up with an unpopular decision. Though ultimately the buck stops with the pastor, the lower-level board or committee will bear the brunt of the blame for its disliked ruling.

Some work a pastor can never delegate to another, but many assignments can be performed effectively by members of the church whom the Head of the church has equipped for their particular ministry. A pastor may think, *I don't have any capable people*. It's remarkable how seemingly untalented and unlikely folk can blossom into competent workers when given a little prodding, job training, reference material, practice and patience. The process of breaking members into jobs may sometimes involve pain, like teaching a teenage son to drive. Coaching demands more work in the beginning, but pays off in the long run for pastor and laymen. People have more talent than we give them credit for, or opportunity to demonstrate. It takes effort to nurture that talent.

A pastor should never exploit his people, but he should solicit their help in keeping with their gifts and personalities. He should inspire, motivate, and create enthusiasm. A youth worker exclaimed of his pastor, "He makes you want to do the job." This reminds me of President Eisenhower's definition of leadership, "The art of getting somebody to do something you want done because he wants to do it."

For a pastor to stay on top of his work, survival isn't difficult if he has helpers to keep the top from getting too high.

4

Plan Your Sermons Ahead

On a Sunday morning during World War II a sailor, driving to a church in Rhode Island, picked up a hitch-hiker and invited him to go to the service with him. The hitch-hiker accepted the invitation. Engaging his passenger in conversation, the sailor asked him what he thought God was like.

"God's like a kind, old grandfather," answered the passenger, "sitting up in heaven in a rocking chair, winking at our wrongdoings, too good to hurt any of us down here."

When the pastor rose to preach, he said, "My sermon is about what God is not. God is not a kind, old grandfather in a rocking chair in heaven, winking at our sin."

Immediately the sailor's friend gripped the back of the pew ahead, and listened intently to the sermon, which dealt with the attributes of God. When the sermon was over, he dragged the sailor down front and confronting the pastor, asked, "Did this sailor tell you about me? When did you prepare this sermon?" Assuring the youth that the sailor had in no way contacted him, the pastor led them into his study. Pointing to a schedule on the wall, he said, "Here's a list of my sermon topics for a year in advance. I planned to speak on this subject months ago."

Years later, after telling this story at a Christian Education conference, I was approached by a preacher who said, "I knew that pastor. Just a few months before he passed away I was in his study and saw on the wall a list of his projected sermon titles for the coming year. Underneath were penciled these words, 'Subject to change by the will of God.'"

Advance sermon preparation will help a pastor survive. Warren W. and David W. Wiersbe in *Making Sense of the Ministry*, recommend working ahead, "It's amazing how more relaxed life can be when you are ahead of your work. It gives you a good feeling to know that you are controlling your schedule, and that you are not the victim of changing circumstances. Once we get behind, everything starts to fall apart. . . . Trying to pastor a church without knowing how to discipline your time is an invitation to ulcers, tensions in marriage, growing frustration, and a nervous breakdown" (71). Though the authors are referring to the entire sweep of pastoral duties, their remarks would certainly pertain to sermon preparation.

OBJECTIONS TO ADVANCE SERMON PLANNING

Some pastors think that Jesus disapproved of preparing sermons ahead of time when He said, "When they arrest you, do not worry about what to say or how to say it. At that time you will be given what to say, for it will not be you speaking, but the Spirit of your Father speaking through you" (Matt. 10:19, 20 NIV). Note that the promise has nothing to do with sermon preparation or delivery, but with persecution. We are to prepare sermons, but not our defense before councils and governors. Of course, some pastors may feel, when they preach, that they are on trial before a bunch of judges!

Some pastors think the Lord does not tell us what to preach away ahead. But if the Lord can tell a pastor what to preach the night before, can He not tell him a week before, a month before, even a year before, as He apparently did to the pastor in Rhode Island?

Planning sermons in advance does not mean they are set in cement with dates that cannot be changed. If for some reason a pastor wishes to preach on another topic some Sunday, he should feel at perfect liberty to do so. The Sunday after President Kennedy was assassinated, many ministers switched from their announced subject to something appropriate for that solemn weekend. You are to be master of your schedule, not your schedule of you. If a special speaker becomes available, you should feel free to break into any series of sermons, if so led.

ADVANTAGES OF ADVANCE SERMON PLANNING

Saves Time

Without a plan many preachers actually spend more time on deciding what to preach the next Sunday than they do on the actual sermon preparation after they do decide. All of us at one time or another have flipped the pages of the Bible trying to select a topic for the coming Lord's Day. If it's not the creation, nor the judgment, it has to be something in between. But advance planning saves all the time spent in indecision.

Encourages Study

Top public priority for a pastor (along with his private prayer life) is his Sunday A.M. sermon. The Sunday morning pulpit hour looms before him all week long. When a student in my Pastoral Methods class came with an assignment unprepared, I would gently ask, "When you become a pastor, how do you think it would go over with your congregation if some Sunday morning you should stand up at sermon time and tell them that you are unprepared?" The class agreed that, if this happened very often, the pulpit would soon be declared vacant. If Sunday approaches and the sermon is not prepared, a pastor has anxiety. If Sunday approaches with the sermon prepared barely in time, he experiences relief. But if he has done his preparation well in advance, he will live in a state of contentment as he anticipates the Sunday morning worship hour.

G. Campbell Morgan said that "the supreme work of the Christian minister is the work of preaching." D. Martyn Lloyd-Jones stated that "the work of preaching is the highest and the greatest and the most glorious calling to which anyone can ever be called." Though films, cassettes, seminars, concerts and drama have their place as teaching helps, nothing can take the place of preaching. So a pastor should put his best work, prime time and top energy into his pulpit ministry. Though it's difficult to estimate all the time it takes to prepare a sermon because of former reading and intermittent meditation on the topic, Alexander Maclaren, one of the greatest preachers of the nineteenth century, was known to spend sixty definite hours in the preparation of a single sermon. To him sermon preparation was hard work. He concentrated all his available energy on his pulpit ministry.

Many preaching giants, including Maclaren, began their ministry in out-of-the-way places. Instead of lamenting the smallness and obscurity of their congregations, these pastors did not yield to indolence, but used their time for diligent study. Even when in a large parish, Morgan, an advocate of hard work, was in his study at 6 A.M., permitting no interruption till noon.

The pastor who doesn't study doesn't stay. Someone quipped, "If he's not growing, he's soon going."

Gives Direction to Research

Advance planning requires a pastor to concentrate on an area of study. Though he will not wish to confine his research to one topic exclusively, he will need to zero in on the series he has chosen for later preaching. This will enable him to select books in the planned scope of study. Frank W. Boreham of New Zealand read at least one book a week. Some pastors have been able to maintain rugged reading schedules, like two books a day, or 300 pages a day, but the average pastor probably doesn't exceed two books a week. I averaged seventy-five a year. I read approximately 3,000 books in my forty years at Nanuet.

Alerts to Illustrations

Many illustrations slip through our fingers because we are unaware that we will be speaking on a particular subject. But if we plan to preach on a certain topic six months or a year from now, our antenna will reach out in every direction, making our eyes to see and our ears to hear, capturing suitable, usable illustrations from experience, observation, listening, reading, science, history, art, and literature. When a sermon is prepared at the last minute, we often hunt frantically and fruitlessly for an illustration to top off our presentation. But advance planning keeps us alert for potential anecdotes which will make our coming series that much richer and clearer.

Avoids Repetition

Dependence on the inspiration of each week may result in a lack of discipline. Taking the line of least resistance, we return inevitably to pet subjects. Or we select those on which we have more knowledge, saving ourselves the inconvenience of delving into new fields.

Gives Sense of Direction to Preaching

If we have no plan for sermon topics, we must admit to ourselves that we do not know our long-range goals in preaching. If we do not wish our ministry to be hit-or-miss, advance planning will force us to examine the purpose of our preaching.

Provides Better Material

When a preacher has months for research in a subject area, the final product should prove much superior to any material dug up in three days' scrounging. A longer period of study permits following leads down many avenues. New ideas will be developed. New bits and pieces of information will be discovered.

Covers a Subject Better

A school teacher has a plan which he or she follows in order to cover a subject thoroughly. Should not a pastor, especially when contemplating a series which involves much teaching, have an outline, and know where he is headed? Should not a pastor be as thorough as a school teacher, and provide full coverage of a theme? A pastor who teaches comprehensively has a better chance of survival than one who preaches haphazardly.

Takes Some Drudgery Out of Preparation

When a pastor has to grind out a production in two or three days for the coming Sunday, and has little material on hand, the enjoyment level is much lower than if he were preparing it without an immediate deadline. Delight, rather than drudgery, accompanies long-range research.

Takes the Pressure Off the Immediate Sunday Sermon

If ample research has been done in advance, a preacher need only pull out his material sometime during the week before the scheduled Sunday, and hone it into final form, rather than start from scratch.

Someone may ask, "Hasn't the sermon lost its fire if prepared months in advance?" I can only answer from experience. My practice was to take next Sunday's sermon out of the files on Tuesday or Wednesday morning, and polish it for presentation. Then, on Thursday morning, I outlined and studied it. As I refamiliarized myself with the message I found my enthusiasm growing. Like the prophet, while I mused, the fire burned. Friday morning I went over the sermon again, also Saturday morning, then early Sunday morning. Each day I sensed increasing fervor, so that when I finally gave the sermon, not only had I grasped the message, but the message had gripped me.

Makes the Congregation Aware They Are Headed Somewhere

At a funeral service, some participating soldier-friends were told to follow the pastor down to the casket, stand for a solemn moment, then follow the pastor out the side door. All went well till the pastor chose the wrong door. How embarrassed pastor and soldiers were when they marched with military precision into a broom closet, and had to beat a confused retreat in full view of the mourners.

A congregation who follows a pastor who has mapped out the territory in advance senses they are headed to a definite destination.

Permits the Selection of Appropriate Music

Hymns, choir numbers, and special music should fit the sermon theme. How inappropriate to follow a sermon titled, "Launch Out into the Deep," with the congregational song, "Pull for the Shore"! George Beverly Shea said, "The singer or choir director should know the subject of the pastor's message and stay on target with the minister."

The proper wedding of song and sermon can intensify the impact of God's truth. However, this collaboration cannot exist if the pastor doesn't plan his sermons ahead. But when a list of topics is given the choir director weeks in advance, he can rehearse his choir in appropriate numbers for several practices.

For fifteen years I assigned my Minister of Music the task of arranging the order of worship for our Sunday services. He always asked to read my sermons a month ahead of scheduled delivery. His choice of fitting hymns and choir music reinforced the truth of the hour and gave an added lift to our worship.

SUGGESTIONS FOR ADVANCE SERMON PLANNING

The following helps are suggestive, not exhaustive.

Always Be Working in Advance

After a young minister gets his first church, before long he should clear some time in his schedule every week for working on sermons for delivery weeks and even months away. It took me a good year before I was able to expend time in this way. Then I was able over and over again to complete the spade work for a series months ahead. In fact, before the end of my ministry, on at least eight occasions I was able to have a book of sermons accepted by a publisher even before preaching them to my people. But I always preached them before the book came out.

Always have a series or two "cooking."

Keep Folders for Special Seasons

Annually every pastor will preach Christmas, Passion, and Easter sermons, but sometimes he may wish to link his sermon to another of the special annual days. So I maintained a seasonal file with the following "special day" folders in chronological order: New Year's Day, Valentine's Day, Lincoln's Birthday, Washington's Birthday, St. Patrick's Day, Passion Sunday, Easter Sunday, Mother's Day, Memorial Day, Children's Day, Father's Day, Independence Day, Labor Day, Halloween, Reformation Sunday, Thanksgiving, Universal Bible Sunday, and Christmas.

Whenever I came across material that pertained to any of these categories, I dropped it in the proper folder, building up a backlog of available material. Naturally, I did not speak on all these special days every year, but when I did, I didn't lose time scurrying around for ideas. In fact, three of my books came out of these folders: *Christmas Sermons, Thanksgiving Sermons,* and *Day of Resurrection* (Easter sermons).

Recognize Three Possible Periods for Series Preaching

Since practically all pastors preach Christmas topics and Passion-Easter messages, many take advantage of the time slots between these major Christian holy seasons to deliver a sermon series. The three months from September to Advent lend themselves to a course of about twelve messages. January to Good Friday also provides a period for a series, its length depending on the date of Good Friday. Then from Easter to summer gives room for another series. One seminary professor suggested for the fall a series to edify, for the winter a series to evangelize, and for the spring a series to challenge to service.

Vary the Types of Sermons

Though homileticians classify many types of messages, the two major types are topical and expository. In a topical message the points of the outline come from the *topic.* In an expository sermon the divisions come from the *text.* If a pastor preaches two sermons a Sunday, he may wish to preach an expository message at one service, and a topical at the other.

I once alternated two series of topical sermons on Sunday mornings. One week I spoke on an attribute of God, then the next on some aspect of worship. To speak on the mercy of God, or His sovereignty, or His grace, or His love, is indeed conducive to worship. The alternating series blended effectively.

Did you ever consider that, if a pastor preached an expository sermon on a different chapter of the Bible every Sunday, it would take about twenty-three years to cover all the chapters in the Bible? More likely he would devote at least two Sundays to each chapter, which would take him forty-six years. No pastor ever need leave a church because he has run out of ideas. Just preaching every book of the Bible chapter by chapter gives enough material to survive. Over the years I have preached expositorily through every New Testament book, including long series on Luke, John, Romans, Acts, Hebrews, and Revelation.

Preach Series on the Major Doctrines

Depending on how you classify them, the theologians list nine major doctrines. These would provide nine excellent series, perhaps dealing with one doctrine a year, either in fall, winter, or spring: God, Christ, the Holy Spirit, Man, Salvation, the Church, Angels-Satan-Demons, the Last Things, and the Bible. A series on the doctrine of Christ could begin with His birth in Advent (December) and end with His resurrection on Easter, or His ascension on a later Sunday.

Well in advance one could read several theology volumes on a particular doctrine, then break the main points down into popular style with up-to-date illustrations.

Here's how I handled the doctrine of man under the series title, *What's the Matter with Man?*

1. What Is Man? (Introductory)
2. Where Did Man Come From? (Origin and Unity of Race)
3. What Was Man Like at the Beginning? (Image of God in Man)
4. Can We Believe the Story of Adam and Eve Eating the Forbidden Fruit? (Fall of Man)
5. The Plague of the Human Race (Sin)
6. What Does Sin Do to Us?
7. Is Your Upper Story Occupied? (Man More Than Body)
8. Is There Life After Death?
9. Will the Dead Rise?
10. Shall We Believe in Hell?
11. What Is Heaven Like?
12. Divine Masterpiece (Summary—Man's Creation, Desecration, and Re-creation)

Handle Significant Biblical Topics Thoroughly

Early I adopted the habit of reading the Bible through in my morning devotional period, looking for just one subject, with notebook at hand to jot down every thought relating to that chosen theme. By spending a minimum of half an hour I found that I could read the Bible through in four to six months, and come up with a hundred pages of notes all on that one topic.

During those months my mental antenna would be alert for secular items associated with that subject. At the end I would have a thick file of biblical and supportive material which I would break down into subdivisions to form a series of six to twelve messages. Though topical Bibles are available which list all references to a particular theme, I had the satisfaction of knowing that I had researched thoroughly, usually discovering references not found in a topical Bible.

I well recall the first time I followed the above procedure. My interest was on the tongue (not the tongues movement but the movement of the tongue), its power and potential. With over a hundred pages of notes, plus a bulging folder of poems, articles, and illustrations, I sorted out the material, organizing it into twelve sermons: the idle tongue, the critical tongue, the gossiping tongue, the swearing tongue, the slandering tongue, the blasphemous tongue, the contentious tongue, the lying tongue, the dirty tongue, the boasting tongue, the complaining tongue, and the tongue's power for good or evil. These sermons became my first book, *Did I Say That?* Other subjects handled similarly included joy, time, money, hope, God's will and worship.

Usually by the time I finished reading the Bible through, focusing on one theme, already another topic had suggested itself, enabling me to continue using my devotional period in the same way. Since I constantly prayed for guidance as to what to preach on, I tended to accept that inward suggestion of the next topic as divine leading. Though many advise keeping study time separate from devotional reading, I discovered that the search for references on a particular topic only served to fire my devotional life, and this almost on a daily basis.

Keep Folders for Single Sermons

Though we do series preaching, many of our sermons will be individual discourses. We should have a folder for these separate addresses. At first, we may keep several budding homilies in one folder, but as a particular idea blossoms into a growing pile of notes clipped together, it's time for that particular sermon idea to have a separate folder all its own.

Some sermons grow slowly through the years. This is why it's practically impossible to tell precisely how long it takes to compose a sermon. As a gardener keeps a succession of plants growing in various beds, so the preacher should keep many seed plots of sermon ideas developing in his files. Some day when in need of a message, he'll be able to look into his folders, find an idea with most of the research done, ready to be preached after a few hours of polishing.

Update Earlier Sermons

Keep your sermon notes. They constitute your accumulated homiletical fortune, like money in the bank for a rainy day. How foolish to throw them away. Rather build on them, like interest on your bank deposits, and repeat the improved editions later.

In my first pastorate of less than five years, I repeated only one sermon. It was a Sunday evening after a busy week at camp. I had prepared a message, but early in the service had an urge to repeat a message I had given two years before. As I stood at the door at the end, a minister-member of the church winked at me, as he commented, "Preach it again some time."

However, in my forty-year pastorate at Nanuet, I often upgraded and repeated a sermon, but usually not till ten years had passed. By that time, half the congregation had changed. Too, I figured that if I couldn't recall the sermon, it's unlikely my people would remember it either, especially if I made some alterations.

Frank W. Boreham, convinced that no preacher could deliver two completely new sermons a Sunday with justice to excellence, always gave an old sermon for one of his services. But he didn't just give a simple repeat. He revised it, and used a fresh approach.

Preach Through the Entire Bible

Dr. Joseph Parker announced on a Sunday in 1884 that he would preach straight through the Bible. Speaking three times a week, he completed the series seven years later. The sermons, stenographically reported, were published in a twenty-five volume set called *The People's Bible*, recently reprinted by Baker Book House under the title *Preaching Through the Bible*.

Other pastors have followed this procedure, but to do so demands the highest discipline and the intent to remain in the same church for a good while. Though I never adopted this plan, I pursued a somewhat similar course on a lesser scale. From the first Sunday of my forty-year Nanuet pastorate I made it a practice to read a chapter from the Bible each week, and to make comment, and to do it consecutively. I started with Genesis 1, then Genesis 2, and so on to the end of Genesis. Next it was Exodus. It took nearly twenty-eight years to complete the Bible. I did not read the chapter on the monthly Communion Sunday, nor when we had guest speakers who needed ample preaching time. A long chapter would be extended over two weeks, and a few genealogical portions (as well as 1 and 2 Chronicles) were omitted. If people criticized my frequent use of topical sermons, I had the satisfaction of knowing that nearly fifteen minutes of most morning services were devoted to the reading and explanation of the Bible.

Anyone attending our church for those twenty-eight years heard the Bible read from Genesis to Revelation and with brief explanation. When I finished the running commentary on the chapter, visitors often thought the sermon was over, and were surprised when later I rose to preach. Some said they enjoyed the reading of the chapter more than the actual sermon. Paul urged Timothy to devote himself "to the public reading of Scripture" (1 Tim. 4:13 NIV).

A reader of *British Weekly* wrote a letter to the editor, "Dear Sir: It seems to me that ministers feel their sermons are important and spend much time preparing them. I have attended church regularly for the last 39 years, and have heard 3,000 sermons, but to my consternation I discovered I cannot remember a single sermon. I wonder if ministers' time could be more profitably spent."

Someone sent in this response, "Dear Sir: I have been married for 30 years. During that time I have eaten over 30,000 meals, most my wife's cooking. Suddenly, I have discovered that I have a hard time remembering the menu of a single meal. And yet I have received nourishment from every single one of them. I have the distinct impression that without them, I would have starved to death long ago."

The Bible is an inexhaustible mine. What a privilege a preacher has in exploring its treasures and displaying its gems to needy people. To find and prepare these treasures in advance, and have them ready for presentation in ample time, will contribute to a pastor's peace of mind, and help him to survive.

Perhaps, the fact that I was more of a teacher than a preacher helped me to last.

5

Be There When Needed

After the last Sunday morning service of my forty-year pastorate at Nanuet I stood in the foyer to greet the departing parishioners. The first man out, from his seat near the back, hurried by me, speechless but sobbing. That night, after our last evening service, the same man walked by me, muttering, "Thank you for saving my life."

I knew what he meant. One weekday morning fifteen years before, Bob had come by our church office and asked if the pastor were in. My secretary ushered a distraught stranger into my office. I learned that at breakfast in the local diner he had told the man beside him at the counter that he intended to end his life. The man, whom he did not know, suggested that he first try to get help at the Baptist church. Before he left that morning, he prayed to receive the Lord Jesus as His Savior.

There's more to the ministry than just preaching. A minister must be a pastor to his people, available at every crisis, unless away. He must be there when needed, or have someone on call in his place. I followed an open-door policy. Naturally our secretaries screened out unnecessary and neurotic requests to protect my time, but in case of emergency, they had the freedom to interrupt. An old pastor warned me at the start of my ministry not to get a phone, "because they'll phone you up." A phone rightly used is a part of a pastor's stock-in-trade.

Pastors get calls even in the middle of the night. The preaching of the Word and the pastoring of people go hand in hand.

Even in a large church where staff members specialize in various activities, the senior pastor will need to have contact with sheep experiencing rough times. Dr. William C. Thomas, veteran pastor and former director of the Doctor of Ministries program at Denver Baptist Seminary says, "I know this one thing: the people will forgive their Pastor for many things, even poor preaching, but they will not forgive him for being a poor Pastor, using that term for his ministry among the people rather than his ministry in the office. They want the Pastor to relate to them, to know their problems, to be available when they need him. This is what counts in the long run. Though I am emphatic in my conviction that the Pastor is charged with administrative responsibility, I am also strong in my conviction that the Pastor-people relationship must have top priority. For this reason, I did some visitation every day, except on weekends, and on weekends too when it was necessary or advisable. I did not neglect the sick, the elderly, the shut-in members, for they are the ones who needed my ministerial concern the most. Administrator, yes, but Pastor in the sense of being the shepherd of the flock, this is your prime duty" (*The Pastor and Church Administration*, 18).

In a day of specialization some pastors may do no calling. But how will they know the needs of their people, if they are always in their ivory tower? Some occasions when a pastor needs to be there involve counseling, funerals, weddings and visitation. Faithfulness in these areas will endear a pastor to his people, and help lay the foundation for a long pastorate.

COUNSELING

I found the following principles helpful in counseling.

- I never turned down anyone who wanted to see me. I came to see that interruptions were a divine rearrangement of my schedule.
- I did not go out of my way to seek counseling occasions.
- I rarely visited a lady alone, except for a few elderly shut-ins. A window facing the street made my study completely visible to outsiders.

When people wanted counsel, I usually had them come to see me at my study. But I vividly I recall rushing to the home of a couple one Monday morning. Their two sons were missing after starting out to canoe across the Hudson River on a windy Sunday afternoon. Later, after hours of suspense, their bodies were found trapped under a wharf on the other side, carried there by the relentless pounding of the raging waves. We had a very emotional funeral service at the church a few days later.

Another time, informed by a concerned church member that a young man was deeply despondent because his wife had just left him, I took the initiative and went to his home. Not finding him there, I left a note. A couple of days later he came to my study and admitted infidelity. With tears of genuine repentance he accepted Christ. Naturally, his wife was wary of his decision, but in a few weeks they walked into church together, all smiles. Their attendance then became regular. They both followed the Lord in baptism. When later they moved away, they found another church and continued in the faith.

I discovered that I often had to wait a while for the person to reveal the real problem. When he or she did get to it, how often I heard, "I don't know how to begin. I am so ashamed to tell you this." A box of Kleenex always handy on my desk often proved helpful. I have heard every kind of problem: divorce, depression, wife and child abuse, bereavement, financial problems, job difficulty, unemployment, career choice, lack of assurance, the unpardonable sin, in-laws, rebellious children, care of aging parents, kids into drugs, Alzheimer's disease, homosexuality, schizophrenia, and alcoholism. I've been actively involved in the adoption of babies of unwed teenage mothers.

I tried never to show shock, but rather to create an atmosphere of acceptance without condoning wrong behavior. If a counselee felt it a blow to his pride to seek assistance, I would point out that there's no stigma attached to asking for medical or dental assistance, so why should there be in pursuing psychological or spiritual aid? When parents were having difficulty with a child, I would often point out that my wife and I had taken one of our daughters to see a family counselor. I might smilingly add, "Join the club."

I tried to be a good listener, even during long pauses. Often just listening seemed to solve the problem. Getting it off one's chest brought relief. When more than listening was required, I never made the decision for the counselee. Rather, I asked questions to throw the problem into clearer relief, so that the counselee could gain insight, see solutions, evaluate them, choose one, and agree to a plan of implementation.

Counseling is often helping another person help himself. I impressed on counselees that the decision was up to them, not me. Especially did I tell wives whose husbands would not come with them for counseling, "Do not go home and tell your husband that the pastor told you what to do. You are the one who must make up your mind. It's your decision, not mine."

Too often when a wife blames her pastor for some course of action, the husband becomes very angry and threatens the pastor.

You cannot win in every situation. Some people, after counseling, will quit their job, marry the wrong person, continue their infidelity, even commit suicide.

Often the loan of a book or article will answer a question or solve a problem. Besides, it can save time and explain a problem more fully. Talking with a Mormon lady who had come to church for the first time, I offered to loan her a book on Mormonism. A seeking lady, she immediately accepted my offer. As a result, she renounced Mormonism, received Christ, was baptized, joined the church, remaining faithful till her death.

When a situation was beyond my capability, I readily referred the party to a trained counselor in our area. In metropolitan New York City we were blessed with a plethora of competent Christian psychiatrists and family counselors. For a lady with serious financial problems, I enlisted the aid of a deacon in the banking business.

I made it a point to keep confidences. Ladies in our church were quite surprised when they discovered that my wife didn't know about a semi-scandal. That gave added proof that they could trust their pastor with confidential matters. My wife, too, kept the confidence of ladies who trusted her with private problems.

FUNERALS

A death in a family makes hearts tender, giving opportunity for ministry at a crucial period. I have conducted hundreds of funerals involving all ages from a day-old baby to a remarkable 101-year-old lady. Several died in car accidents; one in a fire; one was a mother thrown from a horse; at least three were suicides; one a result of a wrestling accident at a high school vacation tournament; two were murdered; and many by drowning, including five victims of the Camp Davis flood near East Stroudsburg, Pennsylvania, in 1955. Several times I was called home from vacations to conduct funeral services.

Six funerals were those of ministers, some of whom had asked me in advance if I would speak at their service, a request which tore deeply at my heart. Deak Ketcham, who with his family had been members of my church while he was Vice-president of The Kings College, became seriously ill at age 51 when Director of Development at Gordon College and Seminary. After my visit in a Boston hospital, he wrote to ask if I would preach at his funeral. The service was held in the Gordon College chapel.

Several funeral services loom large in my memory. Dr. Charles E. Trout, a veteran medical missionary in Africa, spent his retirement years in our area, attending our church when health permitted. Only seven people were present at his funeral to pay honor to this heroic soldier of the cross, mostly family members. As I conducted the service I better understood Jesus' saying that some day the first will be last, and the last first.

In another unforgettable service a mother, who had died in child-birth, lay in the casket with the baby on her arm.

Two of our Sunday school girls, six and eight years old, who lived in an institution for children from broken homes, were mur-dered by a boy from the same school. I had the funeral of the older girl. Her father, who had never once visited her, threatened to make a scene over the situation. So, both service and burial were private with only the father, the school's president, the funeral director and myself present.

When Mrs. B., an adherent of our church and patient at Rock-land State Hospital for 30 years, passed away, she was scheduled for burial in the hospital's potter's field. Learning she had a little fund to her credit, I arranged with a local caring funeral director for a casket and internment in our local cemetery, this with no financial gain for him. Two ladies who had visited her every week for years joined me for a simple service, overjoyed that this lady could be buried with dignity.

More than once I had to break the news of someone's death to loved ones. Never shall I forget one Saturday afternoon when a phone caller asked if I were the Baptist minister, and if I knew Trevellyn S. It was a funeral director from Washington State, who told me that this young man, a lumberjack, had been killed by a falling tree the day before, and asked me to please inform his folks. I drove down to the home and found the mother talking to a friend. I asked to see her alone, suggested she sit down, said that I had some bad news for her, and immediately told her the facts as I knew them. When she recovered sufficiently from shock, she asked for the funeral director's number in Washington. His body was shipped home for a service the next Saturday.

On another occasion, a lady died in childbirth late Friday after-noon. Her husband asked me to go with him to tell her parents, their children, and his mother. It was a draining experience. I was scheduled to speak at a rally that same evening at a church near West Point Military Academy, and arrived just as they announced my name at sermon time.

On hearing of a member's death, I made it a practice to go to the home as soon as conveniently possible. I've been with families in a hospital as a loved one has entered the presence of Christ. Almost always, close relatives have expressed guilt feelings, blaming themselves, "Why didn't I advise against surgery?" or, "If only I had warned against taking that trip."

Usually I had four contacts with a bereaved family: soon after death, during the viewing, the funeral service, and a visit about a week later. I tried to accommodate the wishes of the bereaved regarding the service: music, participants, open or closed casket. One funeral director told me of a pastor who, arriving at the funeral parlor and finding the casket open, refused to lead the service till it was closed, despite the family's wish to have it open. I recall leading a local graveside service for a person who had passed away in Arizona. A picture of the deceased sat on a monument, and trumpet tones wafted from behind bushes.

Most of my funeral services were in funeral homes. They consisted of Scripture reading, prayer, short meditation and benediction, and lasted twenty-five minutes. If music or other participation were added, especially if held in the church, the service would go forty-five minutes to an hour.

Sometimes, sadly, feuding brothers and sisters never spoke to each other during the service. Once a funeral director called me into his office just before I began the service. He wanted me to be aware that the estranged side of the family, who had not seen the deceased for eight years, had brought along bodyguards to show their displeasure at the closed casket. Happily, the immediate family arranged for a viewing after the service.

I always tried to say something kind about the person, even if he or she was not a Christian, but I always pointed out that good works do not save. The hour of sorrow gives a pastor an opportunity to minister God's love to a family. In bringing comfort he often establishes a bonding with parishioners who never forget his kindness, all of this contributing to ministerial longevity.

WEDDINGS

Wedding rehearsals were often frustrating as I tried to bring order out of a chaos aggravated by the indecision of the bride, the inattention of the participants, and the well-meaning suggestions of relatives and friends. But despite the confusion, the wedding ceremony the next day always seemed to run smoothly.

Frequently I debated whether or not I should marry a couple, and later wondered if I had made a mistake in performing the ceremony. I must confess that my policy became broader (and I hope more loving), as the years went by, perhaps influenced by my view that marriage is part of the common grace of God. I never would share a wedding with a priest or rabbi. Surprisingly, many marriages I thought would never make it turned out successfully, whereas some I judged ideal ended in divorce. Saying no to a couple seeking marriage was never pleasant (and not conducive to survival), but most of my refusals involved couples outside the church who were only looking for someone to perform the ceremony. But for those couples I did marry, my sharing in the event often created a link between us. My long-ago seminary training dealt minimally with premarital counseling, so I scheduled only two sessions. The time together helped us to feel comfortable with each other, and paved the way for subsequent ministry to them.

Back in the rebellious sixties couples often wanted to write their own wedding vows. As long as they didn't make radical changes, I acquiesced. Invariably they came up with a ceremony very much like the traditional form with just minor variations. I let them include whatever they wished, within reason, like a trumpeter playing from the balcony, or a relative reading Scripture or appropriate poem.

I recall a new, young couple, asking me to perform their ceremony. I did so, and they kept coming to the church. Two years later I was able to lead them individually to Christ on separate visits to their home. Today he is an usher, and she a choir member.

One Saturday I married a couple. The following Saturday the groom was buried, victim of a heart attack.

Once when I asked the maid of honor for the ring, she whispered, "I don't have it." Though she was a girl full of tricks, I knew she was not fooling. They went through the motions, faking the ring, and retrieved it during the recessional half way up the aisle, where she had accidentally dropped it on the way down.

I once married a couple both of whom had had kidney transplants. The doctor who had performed both operations attended the ceremony. They later had a healthy baby.

One of the heart-warming compensations of a longer pastorate is to dedicate a baby girl, see her grow up in Christian nurture, perform her wedding, then see her later bring her little baby in dedication. A long-time pastorate creates and deepens a bond with families of the church.

Be There for All Groups

On a Pentecost Sunday I selected twenty members of our church to recite John 3:16 over the mike, one after another, each in his or her native language. Situated in the metropolitan New York area, our church, though 90 percent white, is attended by many nationalities. We are proud of a motion in our church minutes dating from before the Civil War to deny membership to anyone owning a slave.

For years we have had between twenty and thirty Jews in our congregation. Moishe Rosen, founder of Jews for Jesus, was a member for two years before he began that mission. Several leaders of the Chosen Ministries (formerly American Board of Missions to the Jews) were members when they lived in our area.

We really did nothing special to reach Jewish believers. They just seemed to gravitate in our direction, perhaps knowing they would be welcome. Cheryl, in her early twenties, came to our church for the first time one Sunday evening. A new believer, she had just told her folks at supper time of her faith in Christ. They told her that she could no longer live at home. I directed her to my study, then brought in from the congregation a Jewish lady who twenty years before had experienced a similar problem with her parents. This lady offered to let Cheryl stay at her home, but Cheryl said she didn't have to get out of her house that night. The parents later relented, and allowed her to stay, though they made a vigorous attempt to dissuade her from her decision. But Cheryl was baptized, later married a Christian man, and is an active believer today.

In my childhood my parents impressed on me that Jews were God's chosen people, and that God blessed those who blessed His people. My mother taught me to show kindness to our four Jewish neighbors. Doubtless this helped prepare me to lead a congregation that would include many Jewish Christians.

Some years after he founded Jews for Jesus Moishe Rosen wrote me, "My life and ministry were greatly changed because of your ministry at Nanuet. Back in 1970 when I joined the Jesus revolution here in San Francisco there was much pressure from my peers to renounce the conventional church as being dead. They wanted new forms and saw the conventional church as being 'old wineskins.' But my experience at Nanuet and your example kept me in the mainstream of the evangelical movement."

Going to Court

A young man who worked at nearby Rockland State Hospital accepted Christ at one of our services. One Sunday he confided in me that though he worked in the sewage department, he was really an undercover New York State trooper, hunting for drug-dealing employees. I took him at his word till a policemen tipped me off that this youth was an impersonator. I confronted George, but he insisted he was a bonafide trooper. So I wrote New York State police headquarters in Albany. Next day a trooper called on me, then the following day George's picture appeared in the local newspaper, which reported his arrest for impersonation of a trooper. When his case came up in a court house in New York City, I was driven there by state troopers. He pleaded guilty to a lesser charge. Because I was present in the court room, even without my saying a word, he was put on probation. He kept on attending our church till he took a job in another area, driving a bus. He seemed to like jobs with a uniform.

Another time I went to court as a character witness for an adherent of our church, unjustly accused of setting fire to his own diner to collect insurance. To this day his widow is a staunch supporter of our ministry.

VISITATION

Someone said, "A home-going pastor makes a church-going people." Dr. Howard Sugden, formerly of Jackson, Michigan, averaged 1,500 visits a year. I had a hard time reaching 1,000. Yet many preachers today do little visiting. So few visits did one pastor make that his parishioners said, "If he comes to see you in the hospital, you must be terminal!"

I classified my visits under Home, Hospital (including Prison), and First Time.

Home

I did not make it a practice to visit the sick at home, unless serious or long-term. I did visit up to thirty shut-ins on a monthly or quarterly basis. One lady I saw in Rockland State Hospital every month for twenty-five years.

When wire recorders first came out, I recorded the Sunday morning service and took it to several shut-ins, returning in an hour to retrieve it, sometimes with the wire tangled in an almost hopeless mess. When later our church had a Sunday morning broadcast, I discontinued the use of the wire recorder.

My first month at the Nanuet church I called on a man, whose wife was a faithful member of our choir. His brother had just passed away. As he accepted my expression of sympathy, he laughingly said, "The roof would fall in if I walked into your church." Next Easter he showed up, and I smilingly pointed upward to indicate that the roof was still intact. I made some calls on the man who told me of his work as an engineer on the Erie railroad. He began to attend regularly, made a profession of faith, and joined the church. I visited him regularly in his final years as an invalid. He often joked about the roof.

Prison

Both newspaper and radio announced that a bank official in a nearby town had been arrested for absconding with thousands of dollars. To our dismay he was a member of our church and former trustee. He did time in the Federal House of Detention in New York City where I visited him several times. I wish I could l say that on his release he came back to the fold, but instead he left his wife to marry another lady. Our deacons and I talked with him patiently, but when he showed no repentance, we voted to drop him from our church rolls.

One evening I was called out of a meeting to visit a man in our local jail who that morning had murdered his wife in their living room, thinking she was having an affair. His two children had attended our Vacation Bible School. Out on bail before his trial, he came often to church. I recall once in his living room when I pointed out that we are all sinful, he replied that he wasn't a sinner, even though we sat within ten feet of where he had shot his wife through the head. After sentencing, I visited him in Sing Sing, giving him a copy of Chuck Colson's *Born Again*, which he passed around among the prisoners. I lost track of him when he was moved to another prison. I can only hope that some seed will bear fruit.

Interestingly, every time I made visits at Sing Sing (now Ossining Correctional Institution), guards searched me, even making me take off my shoes, looking mainly for drugs.

Hospital

Hospital visitation was a priority in my ministry, seeing my parishioners once or twice a week, or even more often, depending on the severity of their illness. This involved several area hospitals, even those in New York City. In later years, unless the patient was desperately ill, I would make my New York City visits via phone. This saved up to three hours, plus $10 in toll and parking fees, and was appreciated as much as a personal visit.

Significantly, several folks I met first in the hospital later came to the church regularly. I would see "Baptist" by a patient's name on the hospital clergymen's book, and drop in. I didn't always recognize them when they came to church, because people in a standing position look radically different than when in a reclining position covered with hospital sheets.

Here's part of a letter from a lady who had been deeply depressed, "Dear Pastor Flynn: It is soon approaching a year since our Lord sent you out that morning to visit a stranger in Nyack Hospital and you prayed that prayer—interceding for a stranger—the prayer that brought God into a life seeking so desperately for a reason to go on living. What I really wanted to say, Pastor, is that I am thankful (praise the Lord) that you were there—that you are there. Thank you for touching my life." Similar letters made me realize that visitation cements a fellowship with people and makes for a long association.

Here are some principles I followed in hospital visitation. I never gave medical advice. Nor did I probe as to the nature of a person's illness, nor give information on the patient if confidential. One long-time member did not want her name in our Sunday bulletin hospital list. I honored her request.

Though I rarely read from the Bible, almost without exception I prayed, including a verse in my petition. I never asked permission, but quietly said, "I'm going to offer a prayer now." Rarely did anyone object.

I made it a point to visit mothers and their new babies in the hospital, often the very day of birth. I also saw people soon after surgery. Though the patient may not have remembered that I called, his family usually did. I also tried to pray with a patient the day before surgery.

I kept my visits short, ten or so minutes. One minister told me that when he was ill, two ministers visited over an hour, leaving him exhausted and sicker than when they arrived.

Twice I visited AIDS patients in hospitals. One phoned for me to come. I saw him later, in remission, at his home. He was back working, but he didn't accept my invitation to visit our church. The other AIDS victim, after my first visit, asked me to stay out of his room for he didn't need prayer. I had to respect his request. A month later I sadly read his obituary.

First-Time Visitation

From my earliest days at Nanuet I made it a practice to visit prospects Tuesday evenings, mainly those who signed as a visitor the previous Sunday. If they indicated they belonged to another local church, I would not proselytize, but if they had no nearby church home, they were fair game for a visit. It was a rare Sunday when we had no visitors. Approximately 22,000 were recorded during the forty years, with usually two or three good prospects every week. I averaged over a hundred first-time Tuesday night calls a year.

I recall visiting parents whose two children attended the primary department of our Sunday school. The mother told me that they were not Baptists, and were thinking of removing their children from our Sunday school. My heart fell, because our attendance had not yet reached one hundred. Happily, the parents did not remove their children, and they themselves began to attend. A few years later I baptized all four members of the family together. To this day the parents are active participants, and their son is an ordained minister and World Vision executive.

In my early years I would keep visiting Tuesday evenings to 10 P.M. or later, till one night I aroused a couple from their sleep. A few minutes of difficult conversation from ground to upstairs window led to a decision to make no calls after 9 P.M. Many times calls seemed fruitless, but paid off months later.

If on a visit I detected a lack of understanding about the gospel, I would ask if the person would be willing to have three weekly Bible studies at home, led by a retired man in our church. If the prospect was a lady, I mentioned that his wife would come too. Many accepted the offer. As a result, many became genuine followers of Christ. One lady wrote me a letter some time after her decision, "I want to thank you so much for coming to my house one Tuesday evening. I could not understand at that time why you took the time to visit me since you had such a large church. I understand now and it has made a difference in my life. This is especially true at Easter time since I am so much aware of the glorious gift the Lord has given us. May God bless you."

I stopped to see a young father, whose wife was an active Christian, to explain the gospel, but got nowhere. I said that I was going to drop by on Tuesday night two weeks from then. He tried to discourage me, saying that he often went to bed early because of his employment. When I stopped by two weeks later, again I made no progress in my witness. (I learned later that he had gone to bed before I came, but that his wife made him get up and dress before my arrival.) One Saturday noon soon after, I received an urgent phone call—he had to see me immediately. He drove to my study, and in tears and on his knees accepted Christ as his Savior. He gave his testimony in church the next night, was baptized, joined the church, and then went out with me every Tuesday night, often having an opportunity to tell his story.

I was once mugged on Tuesday night visitation. Asking directions of two young men in the next town, I was jumped by one of them who said, "This is a stickup. Give me your wallet or I'll kill you." I surrendered my wallet. He gave it to his accomplice, who disappeared. Noticing my hand, he said, "You have a ring." Immediately I recalled that muggers in our area would cut off a finger to get a ring that would not come off easily. I knew I couldn't get mine off quickly. With the release of his arm, till then pressed tightly over my nose, mouth and throat, I was able to speak. "I am a preacher," I said. He backed off.

Moments later his accomplice appeared and handed me back my wallet, stripped of bills but thankfully containing my credit cards and other vital items. On police advice I resolved not to visit in that area after dark. Also, not to fly on the Concord for that would permit a person to be mugged in both London and New York on the same day. I also decided that I should ask the Lord not to give me such graphic sermonic illustrations—I had just announced a pre-Easter series on Jesus and the two thieves.

A couple moved to our town just before the Billy Graham crusade in New York City in 1957. For two years the wife and children came to church alone, her husband disregarding my invitations to attend. But one Sunday morning I saw him sitting there with open Bible, following my exposition of Romans. Next day a follow-up card came from the Graham Crusade office in New York City, stating that he had made a decision for Christ. He, his wife and family were baptized, and served the Lord faithfully till they moved away in 1982.

They wrote me this note, signed by both husband and wife, "We want to thank you for all the love and faithfulness that you have shown us in the past 27 years that you have been our Pastor. You not only baptized both of us, my mother, our children, and married our children, but you also dedicated our little grandchildren. You were so helpful to us when my father was put in a home and we really appreciated your faithfulness in visiting him and praying with him. So many times you willingly visited people in the hospital that we asked you to and I know many times it was not convenient for you to go. I also want to mention the fact that you visited my sister when she was dying and I feel you were instrumental in leading her and my father to the Lord. We shall be eternally grateful."

To survive, a pastor needs to get out from behind the desk to where the rubber meets the road, and be there when needed.

6

Celebrate Often

It was a thrilling night for our church—Thursday, April 4, 1974. Astronaut Colonel James Irwin, eighth man to walk on the moon, stood in our pulpit, related the story of his trip to that lunar body, showed a film of his walking on its barren surface, and told of the spiritual impact of this experience on his life.

I recalled the effort it took to get him to come to our church. My first letter of invitation received only a politely negative response. Later, on a visit to Wheaton, Illinois, I met the astronaut at a bookstore autograph party, repeated my invitation in person, and was able to arrange a date.

The weekend before his coming our visitation teams blanketed our area with literature on the astronaut's feat and an invitation to the meeting. That night the main sanctuary was jammed to capacity, overflowing into our downstairs hall. The audience sat spellbound as he recounted the story of his ride in space, the thrill of stepping onto the moon, and the overwhelming sense of the presence of God during his three days of lunar exploration. He stated that soon after his return he had been baptized at a church in Houston. Though he had accepted Christ as a boy, he had drifted away. "The Lord wanted me to go to the moon," he said, "so I could come back and do something more important with my life than fly airplanes."

The astronaut's presence in our church that night had a powerful effect on our congregation, not only because of his fame and message, but also as a reinforcement of the momentum our church had been enjoying for over two decades. Unknown to us at the time, our church was in for another electric evening a few months later. For two years I had tried unsuccessfully to bring Corrie ten

Boom to our church. An unexpected phone call in October informed me that she would be available for Sunday evening, November 24, 1974. Elated, we advertised her coming through every possible medium, including a large banner hung inside our sanctuary, reminding us every service to anticipate the imminent visit of this genuine Christian heroine.

The crowd for Corrie ten Boom exceeded the attendance for the astronaut, not only filling the sanctuary, but also jamming our downstairs hall, over a thousand in all. She told of hiding Jews from the Nazis in a secret room in their home in Holland, of her arrest and deportation to Ravensbruck concentration camp, of the Lord's marvelous provision and protection, and of her forgiveness of one of her former, taunting S.S. guards, stories so well known because of her best-seller, *The Hiding Place*.

Again, that exciting evening gave our church a spiritual shot in the arm. When a pastor is able to lead his people in celebrating a series of victories, his relationship with them is strengthened. To be able to commemorate conquests a pastor must have something going much of the time. In 1964 our annual church report first carried a page marked HIGHLIGHTS, listing seventeen important events of that year. Twenty-five years later, the annual report of my final year of ministry listed a hundred highlights. While the secretary responsible for the selection included some routine affairs, she showed insight into what contributes to a congregation's esprit de corps, which is defined as the spirit of devotion and enthusiasm among members of a group for one another, for their group and for its purposes.

Lyle E. Schaller in *Activating the Passive Church* suggests events worth celebrating include "implementation of the short-term goals, ... the annual anniversary of the founding of that parish, the organization of every new face-to-face group or class, the acceptance of a new challenge in outreach, the completion of a successful financial campaign, the reception of new members, the development of a new community ministry, the remodeling or refurbishing of the meeting place, the creation of a new choir or musical group, the recovery of a member from a serious illness or injury, the birth of every new baby, the anniversary of the adult Sunday school class, the final payment on the mortgage, the inauguration of a new program on radio or cable TV, the organization of a new church school class for one group of handicapped persons, the successful completion of the vacation Bible school, that special achievement of the women's organization, or the addition of a new staff member.

Every victory should be lifted up and celebrated, and thanks given to God for His blessings" (145, 146).

A church is not merely an endless round of activities for activities' sake. But events like the above have a rallying effect on a congregation, bonding its old-timers and newcomers, increasing enthusiasm, intensifying the participation rate, and lengthening the pastoral stay. Also when celebrating, members cannot be fighting.

THE WEEKLY CELEBRATION

The reason we meet for worship on Sunday is to celebrate the resurrection of Jesus Christ on the first day of the week. At first terrified and unbelieving, the disciples slowly realized that their Master had triumphed gloriously over sin, Satan and the sepulcher. They were so convinced of His victory that they soon filled all Jerusalem with the news of the resurrection. And they continued meeting on the first day of the week, unable to forget the thrill of that first Sunday.

When Mel White became the new minister of a small Covenant church in Pasadena, California, he wanted a sense of exultation his first Sunday to match his theme, "Celebrate, You've Been Pardoned." Two large banners were created to hang on either side of the wooden cross over the pulpit. They depicted Miriam and two women picking up their timbrels and dancing to celebrate the crossing of the Red Sea. Ushers wore large buttons with "Celebrate" on them instead of the usual white plastic carnation. The bulletin cover was a bright yellow. A large paper banner with "Let's Celebrate" hung from the bell tower. A brass ensemble played hymns on the front steps. Though the service contained the usual elements, no one was bored. Week after week people came with the feeling, "I was glad when they said unto me, 'Let us go into the house of the Lord'" (Ps. 122:1).

Music plays a key role in a church's celebration of worship. A study of growing churches in Minnesota and Southern California revealed that most had twenty minutes of praise singing in their morning service. The larger the size of the congregation, the more important music is to the vitality of the church.

I was blessed with the same Minister of Music for my last twenty-five years. An excellent organist, pianist, and conductor, he gave us an outstanding musical program. My final fifteen years, I asked him to arrange the morning order of service, for he had an unusual gift of blending hymns, Scripture, sermon, anthems and special numbers into a unified celebration. He varied the order from week to week, sometimes scheduling the sermon early, with singing and special music consummating the service with praise. Recognizing this ability the church expanded his title to "Minister of Music and Worship." He organized six choirs and ensembles plus a bell choir and orchestra. His choirs sang oratorios and musicales during the year, plus providing extra music on special occasions.

Annual Celebrations

For many years we had three annual week-long series of meetings. Our missionary conference featured missionaries and well-prepared exhibits. Our Bible conferences brought us capable teachers. Our revival crusades were led by outstanding evangelists. When in later years we could not sustain interest for any week-long series, we went to a half-week, or just a weekend or Sunday emphasis. We aimed to have a special speaker one Sunday evening every month. Several speakers in broadcasts that blanketed our area announced their coming meeting at our church. This publicity, worth hundreds of dollars, usually brought an influx of visitors, some of whom were looking for a church and began attending ours.

We had the usual church dinners, annual banquets for the various organizations, recognition of graduates, and retreats for all youth groups. Three hundred attended a father-and-son banquet addressed by NFL quarterback, Fran Tarkenton. Good Friday, Easter, Thanksgiving and New Year's Eve were always observed. Our Christmas Eve candlelight service with its emphasis on music usually jammed the church. For many falls and winters we ran an evening Bible school, usually offering four courses taught by competent instructors.

The anniversary of the founding of our church (1798) was observed every October. My anniversary as senior pastor was recognized annually each February with special celebrations every five years. A major evening of recognition was given our Minister of Music after twenty-five years, and our Associate Pastor after ten years. A radio rally marked the tenth and twentieth anniversaries of our church radio program.

For twenty years our Summer Music Festival featured well-known guest artists on July and August Sunday evenings.

The annual emphasis that did most for the growth of our church was the six-week Sunday school drive every fall my first fifteen years. In 1950 our Sunday school was averaging 120. The first year of contests we went over 200—what a boost to congregational morale! Our slogan a few years later was "303 in '53." Over a decade later in our final massive Sunday school push, to the bewilderment of some of our prophetic students, our slogan was "666 in '66." The week after we reached 662 four people told me they had intended to come but somehow couldn't make it. They looked puzzled when I thanked them for not coming. I could just visualize our Sunday school attendance board, had they come, showing forever thereafter 666 as our record attendance. (We did hit a record of 723. Our Sunday school is nowhere near that today.) We always hired a professional photographer to take a group picture of the entire Sunday school the final Sunday. To this day, whenever these group photos are posted, many adults have fun remembering what they and others looked like as children thirty years ago.

I was invited over thirty times by various churches to explain what made our Sunday school grow. Since every situation was different, I did not guarantee success through our methods, but only related what we did here, using a five-point alphabetical outline.

- **A** stood for advertising. We used various types. One member designed and paid for a banner which he strung up over the main highway through town.

- **B** stood for billings. We booked unusual speakers to appeal to all ages, like Christian policemen in uniform, former wiretapper Jim Vaus, and an ex-test pilot.

- **C** stood for contests. We always competed against other Sunday schools our size. One year we were in three separate contests. The prizes we garnered were minimal—it was the delight of increased attendance and enthusiasm that counted. As Sunday school attendance grew, so did our Sunday morning numbers. We also ran departmental and individual contests at the same time. Some grumbled at using prizes to gain numbers, but I reminded them that D. L. Moody gave a pony ride to boys and girls for coming to Sunday school.

- **D** stood for doorbells—visitation. Because people had seen our advertising, and were interested in our special billings, many were ripe for visitation.

- **E** stood for the goal toward which all our efforts pointed—evangelism. I recall one lady, born in Italy 50 years previously, who came to our church one October as a result of a visit. She kept coming to a newly organized ladies' class. I can still see her responding to an invitation on a Sunday morning the following January. She became a faithful member, and was a Sunday school teacher and president of the ladies' fellowship at the time of her death a few years later.

Every Sunday during a contest we would announce our growing Sunday school attendance in the morning service, as well as our standing with our competition Sunday schools. This six-week period, though suffering a curtailed lesson session because of the contest hype, was an exciting time, and almost a continuous celebration.

SPECIAL PROJECTS

Here are various events which elicited interest.

We erected two new buildings in the first two decades. Giving priority to the growing Sunday school, we first put up a 40-room educational building in 1956. We celebrated four times: groundbreaking, cornerstone-laying, dedication, and mortgage burning. In 1965, after again highlighting ground-breaking and cornerstone-laying, we dedicated a beautiful new sanctuary that festive afternoon with more than 500 excited worshipers. Our speaker was Bob Pierce, founder of World Vision.

The Billy Graham crusade at Madison Square Garden (an hour's drive from our church) in 1957 provided a rallying point. Our people were counselors. The church sent a bus regularly. Individuals drove friends. One night a lady invited her friend, and asked my wife and me to go too. Her friend went forward. She came to our church the very next Sunday, and soon was teaching Sunday school. Later, her husband became a believer, and today both are active members of our church. Months after the crusade people began to show up at church, saying they had made decisions at the crusade and had been trying to find a church that preached the same message. A year after the crusade I announced a crusade afterglow Sunday evening service at which many new people testified of their conversion at Madison Square Garden the previous summer.

We invited Mitsua Fuchida, the Japanese air commander who led the attack on Pearl Harbor, to speak one Sunday evening. How inspirational to hear the story of his conversion to Christ through an American missionary who as a soldier had been a mistreated prisoner of the Japanese. It was also moving after the service to see one of our members, who had been at Pearl Harbor during the bombing, embrace the Japanese pilot.

When a family in our church suffered a tragic accident, our church family rallied around with prayer and financial support. The car of Mike Sonnenberg, professor at Nyack College, caught fire when a truck struck it at a New Hampshire tollbooth. Though Mike was burned severely, his little son, Joel, suffered burns over 95 percent of his body. My wife and I, plus several young couples visited the hospital in Boston to see Jan, the child's mother. Joel survived, but needed a seemingly endless series of painful skin-graft operations. When Mike was able to travel, our couplers club presented him with a check to help buy another car. Jan wrote a book on Joel's experience, *Race for Life*. Joel's return to Sunday school was a red-letter day.

Back in the '70s the eastern churches of our denomination chose our church as the location of their regional three-day convention. Recognizing the honor, our congregation took their responsibility seriously, accepted all the detailed duties involved, and used the affair as an occasion to houseclean our church property. All organizations were asked to clean out their rooms. All facilities were given a good going-over, looking spick-and-span for the big event. I eliminated a hundred second-rate books from my study. Incidentally, speaking of facilities, experts tell us that baby-boomers, now parents, look for excellent physical facilities in choosing their church.

Successful stewardship campaigns, special debt-reducing offerings that reached their goal, the raising of $4,000 to complete the need of a couple appointed for missionary service in the Cote d'Ivoire on the same morning we commissioned them, ordination services of several of our young men for the ministry, the honoring of graduates, reports by youth after InterVarsity's Urbana conference or after trips to Haiti, Mexico or Appalachia, a round-table discussion involving a dozen Jewish Christians, a pictorial membership directory, and a missionary directory—all these were highlights that celebrated ongoing victories.

RECOGNITION

A boy in our high school group with severe hearing impairment was written up in our local newspaper for his running achievements. The write-up was immediately posted on a bulletin board reserved for such items. My wife made a point of sending a little note of congratulation, along with the clipping, to any member whose accomplishment appeared in the paper.

Achievers appreciate affirmation by their church leaders and peers. Among our youth we have had tennis champions, running stars, valedictorians, and scholarship winners. Middle-aged members have earned advanced degrees and authored books. A young man who attained Eagle Scout rank had me offer a prayer at the presentation ceremony. I have attended retirement dinners for long-time church members.

When one of our high school girls went on to an illustrious running career at Villanova, her clippings were still posted on our bulletin board. In the 1988 U. S. Olympic tryouts she missed making the team by one tenth of a second. I would always let her know, as she left church on a visit home, that I read about her in our sports section, to which she always responded with genuine humility. I officiated at her marriage to a fine young athlete who had also been in the previous Olympics in Mexico. Whenever in the area, they visit our church and are greeted warmly.

Two young men from our church were present in our morning service the Sunday after U.S. paratroopers rescued U.S. medical students on the island of Grenada. One had been studying at that medical school, and the other serving with the paratroopers. The congregation had agonized with their parents during the uncertain events of the previous week. What an emotional moment when both stood to be recognized by the congregation and to greet each other—rescuer and rescued!

BE FLEXIBLE

To keep things happening a pastor must avoid going stale. A long tenure may tempt one to repetitiveness in sermons, as well as tend to narrow perspective and limit vision. Therefore the minister must keep alive, growing, and alert to new ideas.

Attending the U.S. Congress on Evangelism in Minneapolis in 1967, I sensed that one of its major purposes was to prepare pastors for coming changes, including music. A few years before, my Director of Christian Education returned from a college course, and played a record for me, commenting, "This is the kind of music my professor says will be common diet in our churches before too many years." Listening to the folk singing, I replied, "Over my dead body!" But at the Minneapolis Congress that was exactly the type of music they played. In fact, the noise was so loud much of the time that I could not discern the words. To this complaint came the quip, "If you were under twenty, you could." Well, that music, and even more far-out styles, are heard regularly in our evangelical churches today. And I had to be flexible enough to change.

I recall the reaction of horror the first time a large drum was used in our Sunday morning service. A few years later a former nightclub performer played drums every Sunday morning, scarcely raising an eyebrow as he banged away.

When I first brought in the Spurrlows, a singing group who swayed to the beat as they sang, several members walked out of the crowded sanctuary. The second time they came, just a few departed. The third time, no one left (or didn't come). Many loud groups have given concerts. Though we have tried to keep the decibel count to an acceptable level, our people have adjusted nobly to the new trends in music.

When I first arrived in 1949, I asked the board to purchase a movie projector. A few objected to movies, but the board bought a projector. Through the years our church was the first in the area to bring in each new Moody science film, and each new available Billy Graham film. We have since graduated to an expensive projector and two automatic screens ready for use in our sanctuary and downstairs fellowship hall. We also have an overhead projector, which I frequently used to illustrate sermons, including a long series on the book of Revelation. We also made filmstrips and filmstrip projectors available to teachers. And we now sell VCRs in our bookstore.

We have members today whose first visit to our church was to see a movie which influenced their lives. Also, things have gone wrong. At a New Year's eve service we had just shown the first of two reels of an excellent film. At intermission during a hymn the operator sheepishly approached me to say that by mistake he had just shown the second reel first. When I announced this error to the crowd, they roared with laughter. Promising that this was the last time we would make such a mistake this year, I then signaled the start of the first reel.

When our Sunday school and church both began growing rapidly in the early years, we faced the question of which to build first, a church or a Sunday school wing. If we chose in favor of the Sunday school where space was so badly needed, it would mean going to a double morning service. Before doing so, I queried a dozen pastors who had done so to ask pros and cons. They all replied that they would do it again, but warned against three major disadvantages: it was hard on the pastor; it created two separate congregations who wouldn't get to know each other; and it could complicate the schedules of families whose children sang in a junior choir at one service while the parents sang in the senior choir at another. We went into the two-service arrangement which worked for the ten years prior to the completion of our new sanctuary. Then we returned to one service. Since I taught a Sunday school class in between, I did find three services in a row wearying. To regain strength I gulped down a cup of coffee before the final service, the only period in my life I drank coffee.

In forty years we had four different starting times for our evening service: 7:45, 7:00, 6:00, and finally 6:30 P.M., changes we felt were needed to meet varying situations. Some churches now hold a Saturday evening service. Many ideas are often the product of two or more people. As frequently quoted, "It's remarkable how much a person can accomplish, if he doesn't mind who gets the credit."

Of all new ideas through the years, the one that taxed the tolerance of our congregation most was the opening of our Friday evening coffee house in May, 1971. It was originally scheduled for our catacombs, a youth area two levels down, set up for informal socializing. However, so popular became the catacombs that the crowds overflowed into other church halls, out onto church property and nearby backyards, much to the distress of neighbors. Hundreds of youth milled around every Friday evening, many of them strangers, often staying after closing time and into the wee small hours of the morning.

The men of our official boards showed great flexibility, and were on hand every week to patrol, keep order, and witness. But discovery of dope, fights, even knifings, forced the church to hire plain clothes security people to mingle in the crowd. The problem was resolved with the coming of fall weather. Only those who genuinely wanted to hear the contemporary music groups performing indoors came. But the catacombs ministry resulted in several conversions, one a young dope-peddling high-schooler who, chancing by, became a Christian on opening night, and later a seminary graduate.

Dr. Charles W. Anderson, when pastor of Brookdale Baptist Church in Bloomfield, New Jersey, did a novel thing. Every late Sunday afternoon for several weeks, an hour before the evening service, he scheduled a representative of a cult to speak on its particular doctrines, then almost immediately afterward went into his regular evening service. There he answered from Scripture the erroneous views of the previous week's cult. This gave him a week to prepare each defense. Also, the timing of the cult message before the evening service gave the appearance of not letting his church become a pulpit for an unscriptural group. That pastor and his church were commendably flexible.

Churches hard pressed to find folks who will commit themselves to regular participation in some ministry may have to be flexible enough to find two people who will share the job. Many Sunday school classes and youth groups are team-taught.

Pastors have to be open to new methods of evangelism. Though some procedures will never change, churches need innovative ways of reaching out. One which proved fruitful came from a local listing of new home owners. A faithful deacon, who was a Wall Street broker from Monday to Friday, spent many Saturday mornings on the phone in his friendly manner going down this list. Though our area is mainly Catholic and Jewish, he would come to me many a Sunday with a prospect for me to visit. Several are on our membership rolls today.

So, for a pastor to survive he must lead his church in frequent celebration. To do this he must be willing to attempt new things. Says Proverbs, "The intelligent man is always open to new ideas. In fact, he looks for them" (18:15, TLB).

7

Defuse Trouble

A middle-aged couple came to my study. Longtime, loyal members of the church, they were disturbed about the new trend in our Sunday morning service. Our Minister of Music, with my blessing, had gently changed the order of worship to the delight of many, and to the displeasure of others. This couple issued an ultimatum. "Unless you go back to the old order of worship, we will leave the church." Then they added this threat, "We know of fifty others who will also leave."

I stated as logically and lovingly as possible our reasons for varying the order of worship, but promised them nothing. And I did nothing. The couple left. But no one else left.

No pastor can escape trouble. Even if he moves to another location, sooner or later he will encounter problems in his new environment. Fairly or unfairly, pastors inevitably face criticism, difficulty, and opposition. Conflict can cause members to exaggerate faults in each other, create a split in the congregation, expend energies on useless activities, and embarrass the work of the Lord in a community. Conflict, though certain, need not always have a negative impact. Properly resolved, controversy can strengthen the unity of a church. It's how a church handles conflict that counts.

The peace of a church is a high priority, though not peace at any price. A pastor cannot please everyone. Often he has to do what he thinks is right, and let the chips fall where they may. To face trouble, a pastor needs a hide like an elephant and a heart like a dove.

AVOID TROUBLE

When I began my forty-year ministry at Nanuet, I was unaware that I was coming to a divided church. I discovered this state of

81

affairs during the reading of the minutes at my first business meeting. The previous minutes told of a split vote in connection with my call. Though I had been the choice of the pulpit committee, a strong faction, at first, gave another candidate more votes than I, but not enough for a call. On a second vote, a week later, the pulpit committee's supporters prevailed.

I soon sensed the depth of the division as people on both sides told me bits and pieces of the story, and cautioned me against the opposing group. I learned of several folks who had left the church. (Most came back after a while.) One former member I visited exclaimed, "I'll never go back to that church. They're always fighting!" (A few years later she was church clerk.) A deacon phoned me after church one Sunday morning, wondering if I had called a meeting of the board without his knowledge, mentioning that he had been omitted from deacons meetings before my coming. I assured him that as long as I was pastor, no board meeting would be held without notice to every member of the board. (He became a staunch supporter.)

Some urged me to get to the bottom of the previous trouble and bring it into the open. But I took the opposite tack. When people brought up earlier feuds, I let sleeping dogs lie. I treated everyone alike. It took a few years, but the time came when everyone began working together. Several remarked, "How rewarding to see people voting on issues, and not by factions."

Don't provoke trouble. You'll have your fill of conflict without looking for it. Don't touch it, if possible. Don't fight every contentious fellow who comes along with a chip on his shoulder. If trouble brews twenty miles offshore, leave it there. If trouble lands on board, that's another story.

Naturally, the preaching of the Word will sometimes offend. I recall a man came one Sunday, but never returned. I had preached on tithing. By the grapevine I learned that he disliked teaching on that theme. Another Sunday, dealing with marriage, I briefly spoke disapprovingly of couples exchanging mates. That was the Sunday a neighborhood couple, who had just switched mates, decided to visit our church for the first (and last) time.

One pastor said, "To avoid all possible trouble I wouldn't even estimate a lady's age." If a lady persisted in asking him to guess, he had a stock answer. "If I judged you by your looks, I'd guess ten years younger than you are. If I judged you by your intelligence, I'd estimate you ten years older."

A major league baseball player, considered a good hitter but a poor fielder, strangely possessed an above-average fielding record. He explained, "Don't touch it, if you can't handle it. They don't call it an error if it's beyond your reach."

A pastor who wishes to survive would do well to refrain from stretching out to trouble beyond his reach.

DELAY TROUBLE

Though some trouble must be confronted soon, some can be delayed. Time solves some problems. Where possible, wait.

Two days before a Sunday school business meeting I was handed the nominating committee's slate of officers for the coming year. I noticed only one proposed change. In place of the lady who superintended the Junior Department was another name. Surprised, I asked if this lady had been informed that another person was to be nominated for her position. The answer was "no," with the comment that someone on the nominating committee felt she should be replaced. I pointed out the shock this lady would experience when, sitting in the business meeting, she would hear the name of every present officer recommended for nomination, except hers. I said it was too late to make this change. Had the committee approached her well in advance, and prepared her, that would have been acceptable, but they could not lower the boom in such sudden fashion. I was not objecting to what was being done, but how. So we left her name on. Within a year ill health forced her to resign. I personally felt that she had been giving a creditable performance. Otherwise, I would have agreed to handling the problem much sooner. But in her case, I felt delay was possible, and time did solve the situation.

Especially in the matter of his possible resignation should a pastor delay decision. If discouraged, he should take time to pray, talk it over with a trusted friend, have a good night's sleep or short trip away from the scene of battle. A hasty decision made in the dark may be regretted when morning comes. A deacon said that in time of affliction his favorite text to help him through was, "And it came to pass." Though used out of context, the thought certainly applies.

CONFRONT TROUBLE

Some trouble, no matter how long you look away, will not disappear. It must be faced. No one in his right mind relishes the opportunity to confront a fellow-believer who stands in need of correction. Confrontation is always difficult and distasteful.

I recall confronting a husband about marital infidelity. His wife had voiced her suspicions, then later informed me that he had acknowledged the affair. At her request I went to their home to talk to him. It was difficult, because he had been a good friend. Though he admitted his guilt, he made no promise to break up the relationship. I had two deacons talk with him. When this failed to change his conduct, the board recommended at a church business meeting that we remove his name from our rolls.

Through the years we have voted out of membership five men, three having served as trustees, for unfaithfulness to their wives. It was never a pleasant procedure, nor did we ever take such action precipitously. We always made several attempts to reconcile the erring brother before taking it to the church. Only in one case did a husband repent and return to his wife.

One young man, in his twenties, was put out of membership because he rejected Christianity to espouse Judaism. How could a fellowship, based on allegiance to Jesus Christ, permit to remain on its rolls anyone who denied the deity of Jesus Christ?

An unpleasant confrontation with a pleasant ending involved a middle-aged convert, untaught in the Christian ethic. Wishing to be baptized, he attended the Discipleship class on Sunday morning. Finishing the course, he came to see me about plans for his baptismal service. Soon after, I learned that the lady in his apartment, who came to church with him, was not his wife. I had to call him in, and tell him that under such circumstances we could not baptize him, gently instructing him on the application of the seventh commandment. He assured me that they intended to be married soon. Then he asked, "Can I still come to church?" I assured him that we wanted him to continue coming. Not long after they were married. He was baptized. He spends much time in Bible study, and is active in church life.

A disagreeable confrontation concerned a college professor who had been introduced on Sunday morning to the Adult Department as a teacher of a course on the family to begin the following Sunday. Within hours Sunday school leaders began to hear rumors of the professor's recent intoxication at a well-attended party. After checking the facts next day, and finding several witnesses who reported other instances of similar conduct, the Sunday school superintendent and I decided to go directly to his office Tuesday night. There we informed him that he could not teach the course. He did not receive the news without argument, but we were firm. Happily, I was able to secure, on short notice, another professor to teach the announced course.

The Bible tells us to speak the truth in love. Without love, truth cuts like a knife. With an overbalance of love, however, truth may be spoken. Confrontation must be done with humility, gentleness, firmness, and respect of the person.

INVOLVE RESPONSIBLE OTHERS IN FACING TROUBLE

When a complaint came about some matter like the change in time of the evening service, I would invariably reply, "This was not my decision. It was the ruling of the Board of Deacons. I suggest that you relay your opinion to the Board." When people objected to the changes in the morning order of worship, I would say calmly, "That's the way *we* are doing things now."

A lady came to my office to explain why she quit the choir. "I saw in the congregation a young man who dates my daughter, and I don't approve of him. Seeing him out there makes me ill. If you don't stop him from coming, I'll have to resign from the choir. And I'll leave the church." I replied very kindly, "*Our* policy is to welcome everyone to our services." She left the church. We could not let personal problems or squeamish stomachs dictate admission qualifications. Don't take the blame yourself. Cite church or board policy. Take refuge under their decisions.

If someone comes with a criticism against another, ask him if he has taken the first step, and gone himself to speak to his brother alone. If he has gone and failed to win his brother, then he should take another and go again. Added counselors provide reinforcement, as well as witnesses to the accuracy of the conversation. A last resort is to take the matter to the church.

I recall a business meeting at which the Board of Deacons unanimously recommended that the church secure a full-time youth minister. At the same meeting the Board of Trustees unanimously recommended that the church not hire a full-time youth minister. I chose not to intervene, but to let the church decide. The church voted for a full-time leader. The Trustees graciously went along with the decision, stating that their opposition was mainly a warning about the cost of adding a new staff member.

I usually took major matters to the church for its vote. Nothing was ever railroaded through. Notice of any special business item had to appear in the two previous Sunday bulletins, one of which had to be mailed to every member. Before calling for the question I always permitted ample time for open discussion. When the staff recommended that the church switch our pew Bible from the King James to the New International Version, we brought it up for a congregational vote. After a statement from the staff with reasons for our recommendation, the matter passed without an audible dissenting vote.

On matters of less importance it may be wise just to go ahead and do them, and not involve any board discussion. Back when the practice was just beginning, I made the mistake of asking my deacons if during the Sunday morning service I should have the people stand up and greet each other. Six said yes, and six said no. I didn't lose my cool, or demand my way, but bided my time, then without asking the deacons, just had the people do it.

Don't Make Trouble Over Unimportant Matters

A little boy was driving with a bishop who became very irritated when the cars ahead of him didn't take off immediately when the light turned green. He blew his horn, and fussed and fumed. After several such instances, the little boy blurted out, "Bishop, do you always sweat the small stuff?"

Pastors should not major on minors. How foolish to pull rank with regard to inconsequential items. Who cares if the Sunday school picnic has raspberry jam or peanut butter sandwiches? Some mountains are not worth climbing. Some battles are not worth winning. Save your ammunition and energy for the crucial battles. Choose the war you want to fight.

I recall sitting on the platform of a Christian college, waiting to speak at faculty orientation the day before school opening. When three faculty members walked in sporting beards, the dean leaned over and whispered, "Tomorrow I have to tell the students they cannot wear beards." As a pastor I never made a federal case out of beards, long hair, or women's pantsuits. One pastor who actually reprimanded a lady publicly for wearing "men's clothing" in a service, told me he wished he had held his fire, because soon after women were coming in miniskirts.

Back in the '50s I announced a series of Sunday morning sermons on "Who is Christ?" To introduce the series I had asked the choir to sing a little chorus which repeated the word, "Jesus" several times. Just as the choir was about to walk out on the platform, a spokesman for the choir whispered, "Pastor, the choir doesn't want to do that chorus. We think it's too informal for a morning service." I could have made a scene by insisting they sing it, or calling on them in the service. But why bother? I replied "O.K. We'll leave it out." I waited my time. Before long we were singing choruses in the morning service. And you should hear what we sing today!

Reading the bulletin one Sunday a few years ago, our board found an announcement that violated a long-standing policy. The youth group announced a car wash on a coming Saturday with the proceeds to help send young people on a summer mission to Appalachia. Our church had never raised money by bazaars, rummage sales or dinners. Somehow, no one, pastor or leaders, reacted. Since no charge was to be made, but donations were voluntary and for a good cause, it didn't seem out of place. At the next board meeting we casually noted that our youth group was departing somewhat from an established policy, and no one seemed to mind. Nor did the event open the floodgates to all kinds of fund-raising. Rather, except for car washes, no other money-raising devices were ever suggested.

On the major doctrines of the Christian faith I would never give room. But on nonessentials I would permit liberty, as on minor points of prophecy. It didn't matter if a staff member was a trichotomist (one who believes that a person is composed of three parts: body, soul, and spirit), whereas I held to the dichotomist position (that a person is composed of two parts: body and spirit-soul).

I lost no sleep over the charismatic surge of the '70s. When I saw what was happening, I preached 50 Sunday morning sermons on the doctrine, gifts and fruit of the Holy Spirit. One series was later published under the title, *19 Gifts of the Spirit* (Victor, 1974). Though I have definite reservations about ecstatic speaking, never doing it, nor encouraging it, I do not fully rule out tongues-speaking as a possibility for today. However, my people knew that I did not wish tongues in the church. I quoted Paul who in the worship service preferred five understandable words to 10,000 in an unknown tongue. I didn't care how often people spoke in tongues in private. I was told that 30 of our congregation had charismatic leanings. They never gave me any trouble, nor did we make any rules against charismatics. They felt at ease in our church, and supported me most loyally. I personally felt that we could learn from their exuberance of praise and demonstration of love. But I did emphasize that we are not to base doctrine on experience, but to go to the Word as our full and final authority.

As a boy in Canada I was reared with strict Sunday observance, and was not allowed to take part in any sports on that day. At that time my parents would never eat in a restaurant on Sunday. So, on my first Sunday as a student at Moody Bible Institute, when all the other fellows dropped into a nearby drug store for a hamburger and shake, I waited outside. But gradually I changed. However, when I became a pastor and heard a youth leader announce in the morning service that the young people should bring their bathing suits to the evening service for a swim afterwards, I must admit I was a bit jarred. Then weekend retreats became quite common, which involved Sunday travel. Voicing objections would have been foolish. How much better to have our youth involved in Christian activity and fellowship.

At first, we would not sell records and books by visiting musical groups or speakers on Sunday. Later, we changed our policy and set up tables in the lobby, realizing that these items could perform a ministry. In my final years we opened our bookstore after our morning service. Kindly, those with strong convictions against Sunday selling muted their objection and made no issue. Strangely, the strongest objectors did not find it inconsistent to patronize restaurants on Sundays.

I felt that one of my critical tasks through the years of change and growth was to keep peace between the traditionalists and the newcomers, who were progressive and full of new ideas. Long-timers would sometimes become bewildered with all the new faces, no longer knowing everybody. They might have trouble keeping up with all the new programs, and worry about their cost. Confused by the magnitude of it all, they might long for the good old days. So I stood in the middle of the tug-of-war and tried to keep both groups in balance.

I recall one business meeting when new members asked for changes in the nominating committee, feeling that the old arrangement resulted in the same people always being nominated for office. We suggested a plan, asking every organization to appoint two of its members to the committee. This guaranteed a more democratic choice of nominees. Getting the traditionalists and progressives to work on a committee or project together helped bridge the chasm. Alfred North Whitehead said, "The art of progress is to preserve order amid change and to preserve change amid order" (quoted by Warren W. Wiersbe and David W. Wiersbe in *Making Sense of the Ministry*, 89).

THREATS FROM OUTSIDERS AND STRANGE VISITORS

Probably every pastor has received a threat at one time or another. I remember a father who had been drinking and came to my study to demand that we stop sending Sunday school papers through the mail, when his little girl was absent. He yelled so loudly that my Director of Education in the next office contemplated coming to my rescue. The man came more than once to harass me about his wife who had wisely left him. His obnoxious behavior stopped when his wife and family moved away.

One lady phoned me from Florida, threatening to kill me, really for no good reason. She had been drinking. Two years later she came up for the wedding of her daughter in our church, and behaved sweetly, as though nothing had happened.

A girl in her thirties, out of jail on parole after serving time for murdering her mother, threatened to kill a couple of ladies in the church, who had befriended her, as well as myself. Apparently she moved away and no more was heard. We did not take these threats lightly, as a nearby minister was critically shot in his study. He lived, but his assailant was never identified.

One threat incident had a happy ending. A lady, a frequent visitor from another church, told me that her husband blamed me for her leaving him. Though she insisted that I had not given any such advice, he threatened to kill me. I lost track of him for years, till one morning he phoned, identified himself and asked to see me that evening. As the hour approached, with no one around the church at that time, I sat apprehensively in my study. He greeted me cordially, explained he had been out west for years, had become a Christian, had moved back, and wanted to be baptized and join our church, which he did.

We had to call the police on several occasions. One involved a girl who exposed herself outside our church office before a Sunday evening service; she was taken for psychiatric therapy. A young man came to the office one summer afternoon, bare from the waist up, claiming to have just come down from heaven. We called the police who informed us that he had just escaped from a children's psychiatric center that noon.

We had our usual share of panhandlers. On one occasion we played along with the police to catch some crooks involved in scams that defrauded churches. They were arrested in our office.

Back in the hectic '70s, our official board even mapped out a strategy to meet any attempt to take over our pulpit during a service. It sounds far-fetched now, but it had validity then.

CRITICISMS

Here are potshots frequently aimed at pastors:

- "I'm not being fed."
- "Your sermons have no depth."

- "Your sermons don't meet my needs."
- "You tell too many stories."
- "You don't use enough illustrations."
- "We need more solid Bible teaching."
- "We need more evangelistic messages."
- "You need to preach more forcefully."
- "Your sermons aren't challenging."
- "You need to take a stronger stand against the world."
- "I don't like the Bible version you preach from."
- "I tried to call you on your day off, pastor. You know, my husband rarely takes a day off."
- "Setting goals is too much like the world."
- "Why reach out for more people when we're not doing a good job with those we have?"
- "You counsel too much."
- "They sure don't make pastors like they used to."
- "I don't like the direction the church is taking."
- "The church seems to have lost its first love."
- "You need to be more of a leader."
- "I wonder if our pastor prays enough."
- "We need to pray for our pastor. He's got problems."
- "The pastor never visits."

The charge, "Pastor, I'm not getting the depth from your sermons that I need," has a frustrating vagueness. In *Leadership* magazine, Pastor Joel C. Hunter suggests three possible meanings. First, the critic may mean he wishes more detail rather than depth, such as the meaning of the original language and social and historical background. Or the critic may mean he wants a sermon to have a clear call for action, application, and accountability. Or the critic may feel a sermon is incomplete unless it makes the hearer squirm under the conviction of the Holy Spirit. Recapturing depth may mean detail, application, or conviction (Spring Quarter 1987, 48-50).

In any event a wise pastor will not fire potshots back at his critic, especially from the pulpit, but will carefully evaluate the barb. Whatever is unjustifiable, he will quietly forget. Whatever is legitimate, he will take to heart and try to correct. Maybe the Lord is trying to say something to the pastor. I well remember, some years ago, a letter handed me by a supportive lady in our church, just as I was to walk out to the platform for the morning service. Opening it up for a quick glance in case it contained information pertinent to the service, I noted criticisms of recent sermons. The sermons were shallow, she scolded, and I used too many illustrations. Without mentioning the letter to anyone (and later destroying it), I took its contents to heart and paid more attention to the quality of my messages. A year later I received a letter of appreciation from this same lady for my ministry to her children, with this paragraph, "Pastor, your sermons on Joseph have been outstanding. Many members of the church have commented on them."

A pastor discovered why a staunch supporter turned cool. Though he visited his father in a nursing home regularly, fading memory caused the father to remark to his son, "Why doesn't the pastor ever visit me?" When this complaint was voiced several times, the son began to wonder about the pastor's faithfulness in calling. After the pastor learned of the situation, he started the practice of sending a brief note to the son after every visit. Then he extended the practice by sending a brief note to the son or daughter of every older parishioner visited in any institution. Defending the cost of time and money on this project, he retorted, "It's cheaper than malpractice insurance."

Another pastor published quarterly in the church bulletin the number of visits made in homes, hospitals, and other institutions the previous three months, thus showing that he was indeed a "visiting" pastor.

Persistent criticism must be answered, else the same fate will befall the pastor that happened to a man who bought a car with a voice-warning system. It cautioned him about unfastened seat-belts, unshut doors, lights on after the ignition was off, etc. One day he heard the voice warn, "Your fuel level is low." He smiled. With the voice becoming harsher with each new warning, he decided to stop the car and yank the appropriate wires. He was still laughing to himself when his car ran out of gas. If we don't heed repeated criticism, we may not survive.

Criticism may be cruelly unfair. A study of pastoral dropouts reveals that a high percentage of preachers who leave the ministry within five years of ordination do so because their idealism has been worn thin by frustrating encounters with church members who are stubborn, selfish, and immature. Instead of discussing matters with the pastor, parishioners either attack him openly or dissect him covertly.

Some pastors have remained in their church by getting rid of a trouble-maker. The late Dr. W. B. Riley, for decades the illustrious pastor of the First Baptist Church of Minneapolis, called this remedy "a desperate act, and should be the last resort. But when it becomes clear that people have done nothing but breed discontent, write unsigned letters, anonymous letters (the lowest conceivable form of conduct), get up petitions and under false pretenses and by foul arguments persuade others to sign them; and, year after year, pastorate after pastorate, have proven themselves ill-contents, critics, slanderers of competence and character, the best thing that could possibly happen to the church is to remove them, and when the time comes for such action, and it is started, go through with it! Don't get cold feet; remove the cancer!" (*Pastoral Problems*, 218).

Perhaps the Lord, knowing that my nature could not take a lot of conflict, blessed me with peaceful people, so I never had to resort to forcing a trouble-breeder out. But when contentious persons came with a threat to take their membership and go elsewhere, I never tried to stop them.

I found one of the best ways to avoid trouble was to keep my congregation at work in divinely directed, Spirit-blessed, Christ-honoring, Father-glorifying service. This engendered a spirit of enthusiasm, accomplishment and unity. When involved in outreach, a church finds it hard to engage in in-fighting. The old Roman emperors kept their legions battling foreign nations to keep them from fighting each other.

And if a congregation knows that its pastor is a hard worker, they will overlook a lot of his faults and failures. A pastor who wisely builds a good track record in pastoral care, sermon preparation, and cordiality to all, though he may not be the world's greatest preacher, will defuse a large amount of trouble.

The author of Hebrews gives good advice, "Try to stay out of all quarrels" (12:14 TLB).

8

Have a Hobby

I never intended to write.

I planned to become a preacher, and shout over the sacred desk. But to become a writer was not in the blueprint—until I met the girl who was to become my wife. I met her late in my senior year at Wheaton College. After graduation, I moved 800 miles to the east to attend seminary, which meant that much of our courtship was carried on by correspondence.

I soon learned of Bernice's deep interest in journalism. She took every course offered in that field at Wheaton. When she wrote me a letter, she invariably mentioned writing. She often spoke of her teacher, Robert Walker, a pioneer in Christian journalism, who was editor of a magazine, *Sunday*, ultimately to become *Christian Life*. The primary reason for Walker's teaching Journalism at Wheaton was to train writers to write for his magazine, for at that time he was authoring virtually every article himself. He began to develop a generation of young writers, who later fanned out into places of leadership in Christian communication. Bernice soon had articles appearing in *Sunday*, has since written 70 articles for publication, and served as Family Editor of *Christian Life* for several years.

Her enthusiasm spilled over. When she urged me to get into writing, my reply was invariably, "I'm going to be a preacher and holler over the pulpit. Writing is not for me." Undaunted, she would send me her journalism notes, enclosing such romantic tidbits as outlines for feature stories and how-to-do-it articles. Sometimes her "love" letters contained nothing but journalism notes, which I devoured with devotional diligence, reading not only the lines, but between the lines, as well.

The next summer I landed a job near Wheaton. Somehow, during a weak moment, I promised Bernice that I would try to write one article during my next school year. Back east, wishing to keep my word, I asked permission of Dr. William Ward Ayer, then pastor of New York City's prestigious Calvary Baptist Church, once my pastor, if he would allow me to write a story on him. He graciously granted me an interview in his office. I took along Bernice's class notes on how to interview, and followed them closely. Back in seminary, after reviewing her formula for the feature story, I wrote the article, and sent it to *Sunday*. Almost by return mail, Bob Walker wrote back an acceptance, and asked me to do a story on the director of the Pocket Testament League. I wrote back a polite "fly-a-kite." I had kept my promise to Bernice. No more writing.

Bernice was delighted when my first article came out, but not too pleased with my refusal to write another. The following spring on a visit to her home in Wheaton, I received a phone call from a *Sunday* editor who asked me to do a story on a missionary executive in the area for a few days. Bernice was standing beside me and could sense the situation. I was between a rock and a hard place. I didn't want to write, but I wanted to please the girl I was soon to marry. So I said, "If the magazine will arrange an interview, I'll do it." Thus a second article came out under my byline.

Days before I was to graduate from seminary I received a letter from Robert Walker with the news that he wished for an article on my seminary's president. Mentally I began to formulate a refusal letter, for I still did not want to write. Then I noticed a p.s. on Walker's letter, "I have written the president that you will arrange for an interview." I wanted to graduate, so I wrote the article, and have been writing ever since. It is my hobby. Some men collect stamps. Others refinish furniture. Some men go down to the basement to their tools. I walk upstairs to my study and to my computer.

For the first fifteen years in the ministry I wrote over 200 articles. Then in '59 I decided to write only books. In the last 32 years I have written 32 books, an average of one a year. The American Tract Society has published a dozen of my tracts. Also, I have had a joke in *Reader's Digest* and another in *National Enquirer*. Both were a complete surprise, for I had submitted neither. Both items were taken from joke books which I had compiled years before, and with the publishers' permission.

How did I come to choose writing as my hobby? Since I never meant to be a writer, and resisted encouragement in that area, why did I change my mind? Here are ten reasons why I write.

Writing Can Be Done on a Part-Time Basis

You don't have to quit your job to be a writer. In fact, you'd better not, unless you want to starve. Most people cannot make a living by writing, though in recent years more authors have been able to do so. Many people we classify as writers really had a dual profession. Ralph Waldo Emerson was a lecturer, as well as writer. Henry Wadsworth Longfellow was a professor, as well as writer. Writing combines well with other professions. You can do it in your spare time. A lady may be a housewife and a writer. A man may be a carpenter and a writer. A missionary, or a Christian Education Director, or a Sunday school teacher, or a pastor, may also be a writer.

During the thirty-five years Dr. Albert Barnes pastored the influential First Presbyterian Church of Philadelphia, he produced commentaries on every New Testament book and several from the Old Testament. When he decided to write these books, he wondered how the care of his large parish would permit time for this additional labor. He solved the problem by doing all his writing before breakfast. By rising regularly between four and five o'clock in the morning he spent the hours before breakfast in writing. By nine o'clock he was ready for a full day's work at pastoral duties.

The writing of my books, one every year, might seem like a time-consuming task, yet in reality, writing took only a small segment of my time. Since virtually all my books are sermon series, this means that all the work involved in the preparation of these sermons had to be done, whether or not the sermons became books. The only extra time involved were the hours required to fashion the sermons into acceptable journalistic form. The major part of the work was done in the basic preparation of the sermon. Estimating it required thirty hours to polish a sermon into book form (it didn't usually take this long), a book of twelve chapters would take 360 hours, or an average of an hour for each day in the year. Isn't a pastor entitled to one hour a day to practice his hobby!

Writing Pays

Grace Livingstone Hill, whose romance novels are receiving renewed interest, was once asked, "How do you get the inspiration to write? Do you take long walks alone?" She replied, "No, I just get out my checkbook, and if the balance is low, I dust off my typewriter." Another writer said her inspiration came when she "looked into the refrigerator and saw empty shelves."

If making money were a writer's sole purpose, it would certainly be a mundane motive. But the biblical principle must not be forgotten—the laborer is worthy of his hire. A writer has as much right to be paid as a preacher.

Incidentally, payment is a sign of accomplishment. How does a writer know if he has been successful? When he opens his mail and finds a check from an editor. Some would-be writers like to write only for their own amusement, hiding their compositions in some old drawer. What's the point of writing an uplifting article if it's never seen by anyone else? But a check shows that an editor thinks an article may benefit its readers.

How much will a writer receive? Though rates for articles are somewhat higher today than when I started many years ago, the chances of getting rich are unlikely. For writing an 1800-word story in a well-known Sunday school take-home paper back then I received a check for $18.50. Today it's probably up to $100. When *Decision* magazine invited me to do an article in '82, they suggested a limit of 1600-1800 words, for which they paid me $150. A book nets you roughly a 10 percent royalty on each book sold at the regular retail price, and a lower rate for books discounted.

Writing does help financially. William Petersen, a senior editor at Revell, sums up, "No, you're not going to get rich writing for religious publications. But the rate is steadily climbing and the eternal investments are bearing dividends at rates as high a ever."

WRITING SATISFIES THE CREATIVE URGE

Made in the image of the Creator, we all have the urge to create. God created the beauty of sunset and sky; we like to paint lovely scenes of nature. God made the mountains; we erect buildings. God made music; we compose melodies. God made people; we create literary characters. God is the supreme Creator; we are creators on a lesser scale. Children express this creative urge by working with building blocks and making castles in the sand. As we grow older, the innovative impulse displays itself in knitting sweaters, inventing machines, designing houses, and in writing articles.

A college professor, after the publication of his book, asked himself, "Why did I write that book?" Examining his motives, he listed six that have driven authors to go through the agony of trying to get a book in print. Then he wondered which one of the six was the predominant force that propelled him.

1. The fifty cents per copy royalty that would help put food on the table.
2. Job tenure in today's "publish or perish" college teaching market.
3. Entrance to the circle of Christian authors.
4. Private satisfaction of achievement and public esteem that results from seeing one's ideas in print.
5. Enjoyment of adding to the world's total body of knowledge, and contributing to one's field.
6. Desire to respond to what one believes is God's will.

He wasn't completely certain which was the prime reason. Admitting mixed motives, he wished he could say that responding to God's will was his main purpose. But in all honesty he concluded that the fourth point was the one that forced him to seek the typewriter at 5 A.M.—the personal sense of accomplishment.

A pastor must have sources of satisfaction in his nonprofessional life, rather than depending on success in his parish ministry to provide that gratification. A satisfying hobby in private life pays dividends in a pastor's mental health and survival capacity.

WRITING INTRODUCES YOU TO INTERESTING PEOPLE AND EVENTS

My neighbor, when a reporter for the New York *Daily News*, held me spellbound relating his assignments, like flying into the eye of a hurricane, covering a plane wreck and murders, and traveling with Governor Rockefeller and President Nixon.

As a writer I have had the privilege of interviewing Christian college presidents, Bible conference leaders, radio and TV personalities, concert artists, and celebrities like the world's heavyweight boxing champion, Jersey Joe Walcott. Because of assignments I learned of events before they transpired and had an inside track in covering them.

One Monday morning I received in the mail two requests from two different magazines for an article on the same person, Jim Vaus, a Billy Graham convert, formerly a wiretapper in syndicated crime. Vaus had settled in New York City's Spanish Harlem, a high juvenile crime area, and saw many gang leaders converted. By appointment I met him at his building where for two years he had lived in most unsavory and dangerous circumstances. From the interview, which moved me deeply, I was able to write two separate articles, one an adventure story which appeared in one magazine four months later, the other a feature article printed in another magazine a year later.

My longest article was a follow-up a year later of the 1957 New York City Graham crusade. This feature, which took major research and much leg work, was broken down into four features. Two enlightening facts still linger in my memory. A personal visit, not just a phone call, made on every high school convert, revealed that over 90 percent were still walking with the Lord a year later. Also, pastor after pastor told of new people showing up in their churches months after the crusade, and continuing to attend, because they had found "a church that preached the Bible like Billy Graham."

WRITING WIDENS YOUR MINISTRY

How many people does the average pastor reach with his message? Church growth leaders tell us that half the preachers in America speak to 75 people or less in their major service each Sunday morning. And that three-quarters of the preachers reach no more than 150 with their sermons.

On the other hand, several Christian magazines have a circulation of 100,000 or more. I wrote forty articles for a Sunday school paper which reached a potential audience of half a million. My total books in print is now nearing the 700,000 level. In addition, some of my books have been translated into German, Spanish, Chinese, Korean, Swedish, Japanese and Finnish.

Communication experts remind us that the printed message has several advantages over the spoken word. It can be read and re-read at leisure, in quiet, and at the convenience of the reader. It never flinches, but boldly advances. It never grows tired or discouraged. It travels inexpensively. It preaches while we sleep and after we are dead. It enters places from which we are excluded. It speaks foreign languages fluently. The importance of writing is shown by the fact of God's written revelation.

WRITING PROVIDES BROAD OPPORTUNITIES

Two hundred religious periodicals require new material every issue. Except for those that are staff-written, this is a wide open market for potential authors. Publishing houses with their acquisition editors are on the lookout for fresh book ideas.

Missionaries can be the source of adventures capable of stirring up interest in the Great Commission. The story of John and Betty Stam, martyred by Chinese Communists in the late '30s, impelled hundreds to the mission field. So did the martyrdom of five young men by the

Auca Indians in the '50s. Who can measure the impact of the *Reader's Digest* story (February 1990) of missionary Bruce Olson's recent nine-month Colombian kidnapping, captivity and exciting release?

WRITING CAN BRING RICH BLESSING TO ITS READERS

Writing is a ministry as much as preaching. One missionary told me that he had received his call through a magazine article. One story on the plight of Korean orphans, closing with an appeal for funds, netted over $20,000 in gifts.

A book on the life and ministry of David Brainerd, written by Jonathan Edwards, exerted a strong formative influence in the lives of many well-known Christian leaders, including John Wesley, William Carey, Henry Martyn, Robert Murray McCheyne, Robert Morrison, David Livingstone and Jim Elliott.

T. J. Bach, missionary to South America and General Director of the Evangelical Alliance Mission for nearly twenty years, was converted through the reading of a tract. As he was crossing a street on a Sunday afternoon in Copenhagen, Denmark, where he was studying engineering, Bach was handed a tract by a young man who apologetically asked if he would read it. Crushing the tract in his hand, Bach brusquely answered, "Why do you bother people with such reading? I will take care of my own interests." He tore the tract to shreds and stuffed the pieces in his pocket.

As Bach turned to leave, he could see tears running down the young man's cheeks and his hands folded in prayer. Bach felt badly, thinking, *He gave his money to buy the tract, his time to distribute it, and now his heart in prayer for me.* Back home, he pasted together the pieces of the tract, and before finishing it, was on his knees accepting Christ. That very evening he went to a gospel hall and confessed Christ openly.

I heard Edith Schaeffer tell how she was deeply influenced by Bunyan's *Pilgrim's Progress*. Chuck Colson was helped toward Christ through C. S. Lewis' *Mere Christianity*.

After a funeral service a stranger asked me, "Did you write an article on Camp Hope some years ago?" (Camp Hope is a ministry, founded by Win Ruelke, to physically and mentally handicapped children in Carmel, N.Y., located 60 miles north of New York City.) When I admitted authorship, he said, "I read that article at home in Kansas. I could not rest until I came to visit Camp Hope and see it for myself." Then he added, "I came in 1970 and have never left Camp Hope." Today David Lilley is Director of Camp Hope, and also a student at Conservative Baptist Seminary of the East.

WRITING REQUIRES DISCIPLINES HELPFUL TO PREACHING

Writing clarifies one's thinking. It forces a person to organize his ideas, and then select the words to express those ideas in the clearest fashion.

Writing forces a writer to an economy of words. A major fault of beginning writers is the use of superfluous words. Experienced writers will go through the draft of an article to cut out unnecessary verbiage. "Was able to make his escape," will become "escaped." Instead of "he ended his talk with this statement," the good writer condenses it to "he concluded." Writing teaches a person to boil it down. (On the re-write of this chapter, I reduced the original draft by 13 percent. Probably more could be cut.)

Writing for publication requires the use of illustrations. A typical *Reader's Digest* inspirational piece usually has 50 percent in illustrative material. To get a written message across a writer needs to use stories. A writer who doesn't use illustrations is like a builder who erects a house without windows. By letting in light, illustrations help explain, arouse emotions, stir the the will, interest children, get attention and rest the mind. A pastor who intends to write articles for magazines must always be alert for fitting "windows." This practice will invariably spill over into his sermonic preparation, developing an illustration mentality with antenna always reaching out for illustrations. Perhaps the Lord could say to many a preacher about his sermons what He said to Noah about the ark, "Make thee a window in it." Writing disciplines a pastor to come alive with illustrations. (See Leslie B. Flynn, *Come Alive with Illustrations*, 1987.)

WRITING OPENS OTHER DOORS TO SERVICE

When as a nearby pastor I was invited to teach Journalism at Nyack Missionary College in 1951, and for several years thereafter, the dean was aware that I had already published over 100 articles in Christian publications. How gratifying to meet former students now active in Christian magazine writing and authors of books. I met a man in a hospital lobby not long ago who after his Nyack schooling went on to graduate studies in Journalism at Syracuse University, served as a missionary in Africa, back home did writing for Christian organizations, edited the NRB magazine, and co-authored and edited the Christian and Missionary Alliance centennial book, *All for Jesus*. As we talked, Bob Niklaus reminded me that his interest in journalism was first whetted in those early classes at Nyack.

Teaching Journalism led to teaching other courses at Nyack College, including Pastoral Methods. I served as a part-time faculty member for twenty-one years.

Immediately after my first book came out in 1959 I received an invitation to speak a week at a well-known Bible conference the next summer. The conference director pushed my book vigorously my week there, confirming to me the connection between my writing and the invitation to speak.

Through the years I have filled around 50 speaking engagements per year away from my church, many of which came because of my writing. On certain occasions I was asked to speak specifically on the subject of a recently published book. I also taught journalism several times at New York Evening School of the Bible, and participated in several writers' conferences. I have autographed books at authors' booths at the Christian Booksellers Convention and the National Religious Broadcasters.

ANYONE WILLING TO FOLLOW A FEW BASICS CAN WRITE

"Anyone who can think can write." A writer should learn the rules of grammar and how to spell. A Christian writer requires a good grasp of biblical truth. He also needs to know the elementary principles of news writing, and compose a few news releases on his church's special events, then advance to magazine articles. A writer should serve his apprenticeship in writing articles before graduating to books. To write a book takes perseverance. Three main criticisms of writers are lack of tight writing, lack of illustrations, and lack of compelling ideas.

A writer needs to get his facts straight—and verify them. Years ago I interviewed a well-known evangelist, who claimed to be the last, living chief of the Sioux Indian tribe. He claimed to have attended National Bible Institute, received an honorary degree from Friends College, and sung at the Metropolitan Opera. A skeptical pastor-friend suggested that I do some checking on these and other claims. To my amazement not one claim proved to be true, except his enrollment at National Bible Institute, which had expelled him. The Indian Bureau replied that they had been investigating him for ten years, and doubted that he was an Indian.

When I sent him copies of all these letters contradicting his claims, he alleged that he used an alias through the years, then penned in "Matthew 28:17" which, referring to the disciples' lack of faith in the resurrection, reads, "when they saw Him, they worshiped Him: but some doubted." I sent him to Bob Walker, editor of *Christian Life* magazine, who had assigned the article and had copies of his claims. At first he insisted that his statements were true, but later broke down in tears, admitting his fraudulent statements. He promised to desist from such claims on threat of exposure by the magazine. Then he seemed to drop out of sight. My wife worried that he might try to harm us, but as a psychopath, he probably felt sorry for us because we did not believe him. The article never saw publication. Thereafter I always checked on unusual claims.

A writer should keep trying to get published. My first book was rejected by Zondervan, but accepted by Broadman. My next book, rejected by Broadman, was accepted by Zondervan. I have had nine publishers.

Publishing your book yourself is not a smart idea. When regular publishers publish a book, they pay for the editing, printing, and publicity, besides giving you a royalty. But vanity publishers make you foot all those costs. And you are responsible for the book's distribution. How does an author sell 2,000 copies to recoup his initial investment? According to a *Newsweek* article, "Ninety percent of the authors lose money, and 100 percent of them know that's what will probably happen. They do it for 'immortality'" (June 10, 1985, p. 13).

Ten years after I wrote my first article for publication, I learned to my utter surprise when reading *Power* magazine (October 10, 1954, p. 2) that my beginning experience in writing had provided the final straw that led Bob Walker, then a Wheaton College professor, to launch the Christian Writers' Institute, now over forty years in existence. Here's what I read, "Walker began to toy with the idea of a correspondence school devoted to helping Christians produce material comparing favorably with secular material. He wasn't fully convinced, however, until he was shown its effectiveness in a striking manner. One day sitting at his desk in the magazine office, he read with considerable satisfaction a manuscript submitted by a seminary student in New York. Unusual, he reflected, for a fellow in seminary to write so well; the article was a product of sound research and clear organization; the overall presentation was extremely readable and fascinating. But Walker was unprepared for the jolt when he learned that a peppy little blonde in his journalism class was the fiancee of the seminary fellow one thousand miles away in New York, and had nightly been writing him what she learned in class. As a result of this secondhand instruction, Leslie Flynn had written his acceptable manuscript. Today Flynn pastors a Baptist Church in Nanuet, N.Y., but he and his wife still contribute to Christian publications, and Flynn teaches journalism at nearby Nyack Missionary Training Institute. That was the spark that set Christian Writers Institute going."

The hobby of writing has helped me survive the pastorate, and is now helping me survive retirement.

9

Learn to Relax

Dr. Paul E. Adolph, medical examiner for several groups, tells of a missionary who came to his office in nervous exhaustion, boasting that he had not taken a vacation for ten years. Now he could neither relax nor sleep. It took nearly a year's treatment, roughly the equivalent of a month's vacation for each of those ten years, before he could resume his ministry.

Putting in long, stressful hours in the Lord's work doesn't grant one immunity from the laws of health. The minister must eat nutritionally, sleep sufficiently and live relaxingly.

RELAXATION

I had to learn the lesson of relaxation the hard way. In my early years, unable to do all the things I thought should be done, I frequently worked till midnight or later, often without taking a day off. In my mid-50's I began to get periods of dizziness. Sometimes I felt so lightheaded that I wondered if I could finish the sermon. I recall leading a session at the New England Sunday School convention in the main auditorium of Boston's Tremont Temple when suddenly I experienced a mild sense of imbalance, but managed to struggle through it and a workshop the following hour.

My doctor sent me to a neurologist who diagnosed my condition as a minor weakness of the middle ear, which meant that if I turned around a few times I would get dizzy sooner than most people. This is why, when I preach, I do not turn my head from side to side. Otherwise, instead of me swaying my congregation, my congregation would be swaying me! Blessedly, in all the years after the diagnosis I never suffered an attack of dizziness on a Sunday or in a service at which I was speaking, though I did have a few mild bouts at other times. Perhaps the reason for the marked improvement was the advice of my doctor—take time off, go to a convention, take vacations, learn to relax.

Too often pastors feel they must be on the go every moment. Uneasy with idleness, they feel guilty relaxing. Every book read must be a serious volume. TV programs, if watched at all, must be news or documentaries. All travel must be for business. Any vacation must be a working one. Some pastors who rarely take vacations point out that Satan never rests. Since when do we make Satan our example, or sing, "I would be like Satan"? Rather, we should look to Jesus Christ Who one day said to His busy disciples, "Come ye yourselves apart into a desert place, and rest a while." Someone added, "If you don't come apart and rest, you'll come apart."

Apparently pioneer missionary C. T. Studd suffered a breakdown because he worked eighteen-hour days with no letup, no days off, and no recreation. Discovering the relief that a shot of morphine gave him, Studd began taking morphine tablets dispensed by a doctor from Uganda. Hearing this news in England, his home board removed him from the mission he had founded.

Muscles keep healthy through periods of contractions followed by periods of relaxation. The bow kept under constant tension soon loses its resilience. A servant of God who never lets up in his work develops over-fatigue which so easily produces disease symptoms. Instead of feeling guilty, a pastor should regard leisure time as an investment in an improved ministry. Spurgeon pointed out, "Rest time is not waste time. It is economy to gather fresh strength. In the long run, we shall do more by sometimes doing less" (*Lectures to My Students*, 174–75).

I am a firm proponent of hard work. But I am an equally strong believer in relaxation. One of the ways I learned to roll with the punches of a demanding pastorate, avoid burnout, and survive with physical and emotional health intact was to maintain a work-leisure balance. This meant taking time to relax daily, weekly, quarterly, and annually.

Daily

Mealtime, three times daily, may be nature's way of giving regular breaks from work. Coffee breaks and afternoon tea have their wisdom, if not overdone. Health experts suggest a brief break, two or three minutes every hour, such as a short walk down the hall to another office, or stretching.

Exercise

Probably the most common daily method by which people seek relaxation is through physical activity. The "high" that joggers experience after a long run is thought to be caused by the flood of endorphins, sometimes called the brain's natural opiate. With less strenuous exercise there may be no sudden high but a gradual sense of well-being and restoration. It is difficult to stay tense while jogging, swimming, cycling, or walking. One psychiatrist told me that he never knew a runner who was depressed. (Perhaps depressed people don't jog.) Because stress delights in a sitting target, pastors need to climb out of their chairs and exert themselves physically.

The neurologist who diagnosed my middle ear weakness advised exercise. At first I rose early to do the Royal Canadian Air Force exercises, which ended with several minutes of stationary jogging. Developing a spur on the bottom of my foot, I was told to find another form of exercise. I bought a stationary bike and for years did twenty minutes each weekday.

Then I switched to walking. For many years now, the first thing six mornings a week, I walk two miles at a brisk rate. Stormy mornings I revert to my bike. I look forward eagerly to the buoyancy of this daily walk.

A pastor should not overdo his relaxation period, like the cleric who was seen for two hours every nice morning on the local tennis courts. Too much such exposure will undercut survival.

Afternoon Nap

When I left to study for the ministry, my mother suggested a short nap after lunch. To make sure the nap didn't turn into a long sleep, she advised me to put my alarm clock in a pail set for fifteen minutes. Before long I didn't need the alarm but woke up automatically ten to twenty minutes later. Now over fifty years later, I still take a short nap after lunch, leaning back on my recliner, and awaking reinvigorated. Many religious leaders have followed this practice, including the Australian author, Frank W. Boreham, and church history professor Martin E. Marty. So have many secular leaders like former Michigan coach Bo Schembechler, and Winston Churchill who napped for at least an hour in the afternoon, awaking refreshed to work till the wee small hours of the morning. He wrote in his memoirs, "Nature has not intended mankind to work from 8 in the morning until midnight without the refreshment of blessed oblivion which, if it only lasts 20 minutes, is sufficient to renew all the vital forces."

Recreation

I have worked most evenings till 10 P.M. I always looked forward to relaxing the next hour by watching TV, or by reading light books or magazines like *Newsweek* and *Christianity Today*. Then I invariably watched the news at 11 P.M. before retiring.

Pastors with children often devote a period after supper to the family before assuming any responsibilities of the evening. Leisure experts recommend that each day include some time working on a creative project, perhaps one's hobby.

With my study at church, I was able to leave my work behind when I came home, separating myself from my occupation.

Weekly

Every pastor should loaf one day a week. I rested Monday, after the hectic duties of Sunday. Some prefer to gather up loose ends on Monday, so take another day, like Thursday. Some store up energy for Sunday by taking off Saturday, which also enables them to spend time with their children on an off-school day. Others take a half-Saturday and a half-Monday.

The busier a pastor, the more imperative this weekly change. The Israelites, who failed to rest from their agricultural tasks on their day of rest, thought they were saving time. But after several centuries of sabbath-breaking, they suffered seventy years of Babylonian captivity when they couldn't work their fields. Neither can a minister work seven days a week without penalty. Unless he relaxes one day out of seven, overwork will overtake him. A pastor needs a radical change of pace weekly.

Dr. Martyn Lloyd-Jones, who kept up his interest in medicine after he became a pastor, said that some would be surprised at one of his reading habits in the ministry. He said, "I have made it my custom throughout the years to read on Saturday nights the *British Medical Journal*. Let me explain why I made this my practice. I used to prepare sermons on Fridays and Saturdays. When I have thought over material in this way, my mind tends to be overactive with it. So I had to find something which would divert my mind to more leisurely pursuits. . . . It worked!"

I gave much of Monday, my day off, to my wife, and also to my children after school, often taking them somewhere, and almost always playing games with them in the evening. I also reserved Thursday evenings to take my wife out for an inexpensive meal. This time together every week was vital and relaxing.

Quarterly

When our daughters were growing up, we had to take my month's vacation in the summer. Who else but grandparents would have us with seven daughters? So we spent two weeks with my folks in Canada, and two weeks with my wife's folks in Illinois. Taking vacation all at once meant eleven months without a break, often leaving me wondering if I could make it to the next summer.

But when the children were older, and the church increased our vacation to six weeks a year, we arranged to spread our holidays throughout the year, trying to get away every two or three months. Every winter my wife and I began attending the annual conventions of the National Religious Broadcasters in Washington, and of the National Association of Evangelicals, whenever it convened. If these were held near a vacation spot, like Orlando, we would stay a few extra days near Disney World. In later years the church paid my expenses to our annual denominational meeting. Again, we often extended our stay for sightseeing. For example, after a convention in San Diego, we motored with friends up the scenic California coast to San Francisco. After a convention in Oregon, we took in Banff, Lake Louise, and Jasper Park in the Canadian Rockies. Also, after a speaking engagement, we might extend our visit for a few days of rest. By combining business with pleasure we were able to manage several short vacations.

Annually

Even if a pastor is able to get away for a few days every few months, he should take a longer holiday every year. A congregation should not expect its pastor to be continually profound week after week, year after year, without periods of extended holidays. No pastor should feel guilty about a long vacation. Look at it this way: The sixty hours a week a minister works in eight months equals the same amount of time as a forty-hour-a-week worker in twelve months. If the minister works four months more each year than most employees, it would seem that he is entitled to at least one month's vacation.

Some large churches give their pastors the entire summer off, a time devoted to rest, study and sermon planning. When Leonardo da Vinci was painting *The Last Supper*, observers were critical of the long periods when he would just sit in the cloister and mediate. He would reply, "When I pause the longest, I make the most telling strokes." Pauses from intensive periods of hard work will refresh, reduce oversensitivity, fill us with gratitude, renew us for our daily work, and enable us to make our most telling strokes. In other words—help us to survive.

Variety

One advantage of the ministry is its wide variety of duties. A pastor need not be stuck at a desk all day, but one may enjoy the freedom of diverse activities. One may spend most of the morning in the study, part of the afternoon in visiting, and some evening hours in administrative work.

Additional variety is possible. In my case, I taught at Nyack College, filled an average of fifty outside speaking engagements a year, and broadcast a weekly radio program.

Teaching at Nyack College

Two years after my arrival in Nanuet I was invited to teach Journalism at Nyack College, five miles away. A few years later, before the Christian and Missionary Alliance had a seminary, I was asked to teach Pastoral Methods to those headed for the pastorate. I served as a part-time faculty member for twenty-one years (1951–1972). The Dean graciously scheduled my courses at the 7:50 A.M. period, enabling me to be back in my study by 9:00 A.M., thus giving the church a full day's work. Usually I taught just one course a semester, involving only two mornings a week, and did not get enmeshed in any faculty meetings or duties. Though teaching meant more work, I found interaction with young minds stimulating. Two of my books grew out of my teaching: *How to Save Time in the Ministry* and *Come Alive with Illustrations*.

Speaking Engagements

All through the years, I filled an average of 30 to 50 speaking engagements a year away from my church at banquets, rallies, seminars, weekend Bible conferences, retreats, and college chapel services. Since 1960 I spoke every summer at one to three Bible conferences. I constantly prayed, "Lord, please don't send me more invitations than I can fill— just the ones You wish me to take." Remarkably, I was able to fill most of the requests.

Speaking engagements have involved a series of services at several schools including Gordon College, the Conservative Baptist Seminaries at both Denver and Portland, the Bible Institute of New England, The Kings College, Bethel College (Founders' Week), and Moody Bible Institute (Pastors' Conference).

I found travel relaxing. Rarely was new sermon preparation

required, since I updated old sermons. Freedom from phones provided relief. Many are the times I have spoken at Nanuet on a Sunday summer morning, then immediately jumped in the car with a bag lunch to drive up to 300 miles to begin a series of meetings that same evening at a Bible conference. Or I have hurried to the airport to fly somewhere for the same reason. The frequent change of scenery helped me survive the routine at Nanuet.

Radio

At the age of nineteen, as a first-year student at Moody Bible Institute, I was hired by the school's radio station, WMBI, to write continuity, and I earned my way through the rest of my three-year course. Taking the first class ever offered in Radio Broadcasting offered at Moody, taught by Wendell P. Loveless, aroused a permanent interest in Christian radio. Though opportunities to broadcast occurred frequently, not till a new station, WRKL, opened in our county in 1965 did our church sponsor a regular paid weekly program, *Focus*. In the next two years, two Christian stations, WFME, the metropolitan New York area outlet of the Family Network, and WIHS in Connecticut, asked to carry the program on a sustaining basis.

Our church radio committee decided never to ask for money. During the twenty-four years of my radio ministry the church paid for *Focus*. I scripted the talk and offered it free to the public. Over 400 requests were received annually for many years. People could never seem to spell my name correctly, so letters reached me addressed to Finn, Flum, deFleng, Flint, Flem, Flamm, Errol Flynn, Fleming, Flinch, Dr. Slim, Leslie B. Flat, Fling, Dr. Leslie Beefland, Fleen, Flank, Flakey, and Flunet from Minuet.

To attract the unbeliever we decided to begin the program with a nonreligious approach. Avoiding mention of anything Christian, the introductory chat referred to some current, secular matter. But when I reached the main section, the material always became scriptural and spiritual. At first, our church folk didn't understand our approach. They thought we were wasting money with the opening non-Christian material. But soon most came to see the wisdom of beginning with a neutral approach when nonchurch friends told them how the program caught their attention at the start and kept them listening, unsuspectingly, to what really became a sermon.

We handled controversial, current topics like homosexuality, abortion, the new morality, gambling, drugs, pornography, astrology, pre- and extramarital sex. I managed to get mileage out of many sermons, first preaching them in church, then fashioning them into a radio talk, then using them for outside speaking engagements, then perhaps as a chapter in a book. My only part in the radio ministry was the preparation and delivery of the talk. The taping, engineering, announcements, selection of music, editing, mailing of tapes, and correspondence were all handled by others.

We received ample evidence that our approach was effective. For example, after we had the Japanese Air Commander who led the attack on Pearl Harbor speak in our church, the following ad, one column wide and six inches deep, appeared two days running in the *New York Times* headed, "So Sorry, Please. We Forgot Pearl Harbor." It read, "A church in Nanuet, N.Y., recently exercised its prerogative of forgiveness by inviting a former Japanese air force captain as a guest speaker to reminisce about his experiences leading a squadron of Japanese planes to bomb Pearl Harbor. O.K., so let's forget the people who became very dead, very crippled, very widowed, very orphaned. While we're at it, let's also forget the Philippines, Corregidor, Wake Island, Iwo Jima and other such tourist attractions. Now that the game is over, let's all sit back together and be Monday morning quarterbacks and talk over all the good old days that resulted in murder for millions of people. I wonder if the Jewish community in Rockland county would invite a former Nazi who turned on the jets in the gas chambers and welcome him for an evening of reminiscence and small talk. We doubt it." It was signed by the president of an advertising agency in the next town.

I went to see the advertiser and learned that the ad, costing $300 for each insertion in the *New York Times*, was a publicity stunt. When I asked how he knew about the Japanese air commander speaking in our church, he answered, "Oh, I heard it on your radio program. I listen every week, and you always trap me by your introductions."

Many listened who would never come to our church. A social studies' teacher in our high school invited me to address his class. As we walked down the hall to his room, he said, "One Sunday morning I happened to catch you, just before going out the door for mass. I made my family come back in. From that Sunday on, we attended a later mass." I received requests for the talks from priests, nuns and rabbis.

Several new members came as a result of the broadcast. Looking out at the congregation one Sunday it dawned on me that two of the ushers that morning had found our church because of *Focus*. Some said that they had listened to the program ten years before getting the courage to visit our church.

The program seemed to have an effect on two of the station's announcers. The first one, back in the '70s, sent me a six-page handwritten letter to let me know that for years the only sermon he heard was my *Focus* talk, and that as as a result he was now back serving in his church. The year before I retired, a stranger, leaving the morning service, said, "You don't know me, but I would know your voice anywhere. I am an announcer at WRKL. For four years I have put your show on the air. At first, I had no interest in such matters. Then you began to arouse my curiosity. Before long I arranged all my work so I could listen without interruption. I want you to know that mainly because of your broadcast, I am now a believer in the Lord Jesus." Though he lives in New York City, he often drops by to see me. Both announcers told their story from our church pulpit.

The variety of radio and the anticipation of its potential outreach constantly buoyed my spirits and contributed to my survival.

AVOID PERFECTIONISM

A pastor's task is so comprehensive that, if he were to work day and night, he could never accomplish all he would like to do. Unless he accepts his limitations, this state of incompletion can be disastrous to the perfectionist, and agonizing to the conscientious. The saintly Andrew Bonar often expressed regrets over past failures. Alexander Maclaren would often feel that his sermons fell below par, at the same time lamenting that he did his best. Both men were idealists. An astute member once said to me, "You preachers have an impossible job—to come up with a winner every Sunday morning." Though improvement and excellence should be our goals, every sermon cannot be a masterpiece.

No pastor wins every battle. Some suggestions will be rejected. Some motions will be voted down. He cannot always have his way. I had to learn not to be on the defensive. The moment a pastor gives up his need to have control, his opponents often begin to relax, listen, and may even change their thinking.

Some members will move away. Some will leave and go to another church. But some will come to you by leaving another church. Somehow it all balances out. (Too bad our churches can't have an annual "trade day" when we do all our member-swapping at one time.) When a church is small, visitors say they want a bigger church. When a church is big, people say they want a smaller fellowship. You can't win 'em all!

Some people have returned a few years after joining another church. We remain friends with those who leave permanently. One couple, who lived three towns away, left because they wanted their son to go to the same church as his school pals. We esteem them highly, the father having served as chairman of our deacons, and the mother as a church secretary. A few summers ago when I arrived to speak at a summer Bible conference a hundred miles away, we found them a couple of cabins away, surprising us as conference guests for the week. As we visit nearby churches in our retirement, former members greet us warmly. Recently during visitor-greeting in a morning service, a former worker introduced me as "the man who led me to the Lord thirty years ago." My wife refers to former members in other churches as "our missionaries."

Everyone makes mistakes. So what? One Sunday evening, as I stood in the baptistry about to conduct a baptismal service, I began to intone the start of the communion service, "The same night in which he was betrayed. . . ." Realizing my mistake, I switched to the proper words. I went on as though nothing had happened, relieved that I had not gone farther into the communion formula. Ten years later I met a lady who said, "I was in your church just once. That was the night you started the communion service in the baptistry!" We shouldn't agonize over errors, but just plug on.

If some of our board members or teachers fail in some aspect of their duties, ponder the good things they do, and be thankful. You work with what you have—with people's strengths. You work around their weaknesses, and move forward.

HAVE A LAUGH

Abraham Lincoln, whose laugh was like the neigh of a wild horse, once said, "If I didn't laugh with the strain that is on me night and day, I should go mad." In our hectic age few prescriptions are as inexpensive and as potent as the wonder drug of laughter. A doctor said, "If you can't take a joke, you'll have to take medicine." Sounds like the Bible verse, "A merry heart doeth good like a medicine" (Prov. 17:22). Another doctor observed that cheerful people resist disease better than glum folk, adding, "The surly bird catches the germ." The pastor who appreciates humor and enjoys a good laugh will find it relaxing, and helpful to his ministerial survival.

In his book, *The Anatomy of an Illness*, Norman Cousins claimed that laughter played a major part in his recovery from serious illness. He calls laughing "internal jogging." Laughter seems to influence all body systems including heart muscles, circulation, lungs, respiration, brain and central nervous systems. According to an American Medical Association bulletin, research indicates that every organ of the body responds to laughter for our good. Humor gives us pleasure, helps us recover perspective, opens our minds to new viewpoints, and releases us from stress.

Psychologists also tell us that the negative emotions of anger, resentment, fear and depression can be modified by laughter. Norman Cousins' laughter-and-healing discoveries are now taught in several medical colleges. He claimed that ten minutes of belly laughter gave him two hours of pain-free sleep.

Humor helps us live above the trivial, and not to take ourselves and our circumstances too seriously. Seeing the funny side of things may rescue us from unbalanced tenseness and hysteria, keep us sane, and help us laugh the trouble away.

Mirth saturated their lives so much that more than once David Livingstone said to his wife, "Really, my dear, we ought not to indulge in so many jokes. We are getting too old. It is not becoming. We must be more staid."

Luther once declared that he did not wish to go to heaven if God did not understand a joke. John Calvin had a fine sense of humor, made good puns, and laughed with his friends. Spurgeon's lectures to his ministerial students are filled with humor. When rebuked for using so much humor in the pulpit, Spurgeon replied, "Well, madam, you may very well be right; but if you knew how much I held back, you would give me more credit than you are giving me now!" D. L. Moody was full of fun and good humor. He could toss back his head, laugh till he rocked, even wiping the tears from his eyes. It is said that he liked to gather his associates around him at the close of day to see who had the best story to tell. When a lady once asked him how he could laugh not long after preaching a solemn sermon, he replied, "If I didn't, I'd have a nervous breakdown at the pace at which I live."

With an Irish name like Flynn, understandably I enjoy humor. As I heard one pulpiteer say, "When peoples' mouths are open with laughter, I pour down doses of truth." No one knows the humor I've restrained in the pulpit, probably wisely.

But I've used humor to defuse tense situations in church business meetings. One night after a very close vote, I said, "That vote was like your face. Your ayes (eyes) are above your no's (nose)."

Everyone laughed, and you could feel the intensity diminish.

After he left the White House a senator said to President Harry Truman, "I'm glad the president hasn't lost his sense of humor." Truman replied, "Any man who has the job I've had, and didn't have a sense of humor wouldn't still be here."

He who laughs—lasts.

10

Help Your Family Make It
by Bernice Flynn

In this chapter, I would like to share with you some factors that helped us survive as a couple, and as a family, and helped me survive as an individual.

AS A COUPLE

"Do you love me?" I repeatedly asked Les. He would frown and give me a "what nonsense" look. Aloud he would say, "Of course I love you." I pursued the subject. "Do you really love me?" The question was raised too often for his comfort, so he mentioned it to a visiting Bible teacher. The wise man asked about Les's schedule. "What she is saying is, 'If you loved me, you would give me more time.' I advise you to set aside one evening a week as a date night, and keep it as sacred as your other obligations." That was the beginning of our Thursday evening escape nights.

I dressed in my most becoming outfit and did not bring up household subjects. We needed to realize that we had been talking to each other, but not listening. *Communication* soon came to be a key element of our survival as a couple. As the years go by we now find that a word will communicate more than a paragraph. Les does not like cucumbers, so if there is something distasteful, all he has to say is "cucumber." When we were discussing something I didn't want the children to overhear, I'd say, "The room hasn't been swept." After our main meal Les will often give me a hug and a verbal "Thank you for another lovely dinner." Out of the blue he'll squeeze my hand and smile at me. It communicates to me that I am cherished. Sometimes when I share a problem with Les, he'll say, "Let's solve it," and give solutions. But I just want him to listen and understand how I am feeling.

His parents were good mentors. When his parents, in their eighties, were visiting us one Christmas time, as they were getting out of our car after the midnight service, his mother began to slip on the icy pavement. She called out, "Jim, I'm falling." His father answered, "Fall into my arms, Agnes."

If something bothers me, I am quick to let Les know it. Sharing has been more difficult for Les, because his only sibling was thirteen years older, and he never had anyone near his age with whom to practice arguing. He seldom loses his cool, or says things he later regrets. I have had to learn not to say, "You are too time conscious." I make quick decisions, and it irritated me when Les took time to think things out logically and carefully. We have come to learn that little irritations are best brought into the open, i.e.: Les didn't like the way I put the receiver on the phone hook; I don't like to eat dessert until the table has been cleared.

Our best sharing time seemed to be late at night and in our bedroom. The children were asleep. No phone or doorbell rang. We shared our weaknesses and failures. We bragged about successes, and we prayed together. One night I awoke screaming. Les turned to me, "What's the matter?" I panted, "I had a nightmare. A man was chasing me." Les said, "Aren't you thankful that you're attractive enough that a man wants to chase you?"

In addition to communication we survived because of *partnership*. One night Les came home late and eagerly told me how he was able to explain the plan of salvation to a man who then accepted the Lord. I was envious. He was out in the exciting world. I was home with the children. Sensing my feeling, he put his arm around me, "You were a part of it. It would not have been possible, if you had not freed me to do it."

A pastor and wife received this card on their thirtieth wedding anniversary. "To dad who for 30 years ruled the roost. To mom who for thirty years ruled the rooster." In reality, as their children well knew, togetherness and mutual submission were key ingredients in their marriage.

Some matters I left to Les to decide. Through the years he received invitations to consider moving to another church. Though he would dialogue with me on the possibility, I would defer to him for the decision. Similarly, I would discuss items that related to the decoration of the parsonage with him, but final choice would be mine. To save him time I handled the bills, wrote the checks, and balanced the checkbook. After his retirement I joyfully gave these jobs to him.

Les and I have had to learn to accept differences in each other. I am gregarious. Wherever I go, I join in conversations and make friends, whether in a department store, at a Bible conference, or on vacation. Les has come to accept the fact that these new people may join our circle of friends and receive an invitation to our home.

I enjoy gift shops. Les does not like to gift-shop. I seldom needed or wanted what he did buy. One birthday he decided to write out promises like, "I will take you out to dinner," or "You can go to the department store and spend $50." He hid the slips of paper and I had to hunt for them. He saw my delight and has continued the practice.

At shopping centers we go our separate ways, and meet later. I take short trips with friends, or on my own, some spur-of-the-moment.

One snowy December morning the phone rang in our Nanuet, New York parsonage. The call was from a friend in Grosse Point, Michigan, "I'm putting the finishing touches to my annual smorgasbord. I wish you could be here." So did I, when I recalled the elegant spreads she would lay when she lived in New Jersey, near us. As I hung up the phone, the doorbell rang. It was our daughter. I told her with whom I had been talking, and how she wished I could be at her party that night. "Why don't you go? I'll make the plane reservation while you pack." You can imagine my friend's amazement when I greeted her at party time that same evening.

I accept Les's limitations. His father was not handy around the house, and he inherited that gene. In our first home he put up the curtain brackets. The man who came to install shades asked who had put up the brackets. Proudly I said, "My husband!" He sighed, "Lady, when you put up the curtains, you're going to have a problem. These brackets are upside down." I made a decision. I said to Les, "Forget the house. Write books."

Acceptance involves forgiveness. Because we know ourselves as vulnerable, flawed, weak human beings, we realize that our mates are similar, and so we should have compassion.

Les and I try to encourage and inspire each other to elevations of achievement. Les mentors me spiritually. I try to keep him up to date on modern trends and culture. I haul him to museums. We didn't hesitate to leave our growing family to take overseas trips or attend conferences in this country. We once left a six-week-old baby for a three-day editorial conference. We gave our marriage relationship priority over parenthood, believing if we were good mates, we would be better parents. Dr. Quentin Hyder, a Christian psychiatrist in the metropolitan New York area, gave this advice in a family workshop in our church: *parents should pray together daily for their children by name.*

Growth is a deliberate choice. Picking new activities to do together kindles excitement. One afternoon in Hawaii Les was planning to lie by the pool. I persuaded him to follow me to the hotel's athletic club into the steam room for a sauna, then to a shower, then to the whirlpool, then to an outdoor pool which, as you swam across, led under a spraying waterfall to another pool with a cave on one side, which contained a semi-hidden whirlpool and a refreshment area. This new experience was more enjoyable than the usual reclining by the pool.

Marital difficulties should not be talked over with friends unless you want your problems to become common knowledge. I was once with a group of ladies who began to discuss their husbands' faults. As we approached the dessert table, I said to one of the ladies, "I noticed that you were silent during the discussion." She smiled, "My husband has no faults." As a young minister's wife, I learned a valuable lesson that day.

It helps to have the same dreams, goals, and shared vision. In his address at the marriage of the Prince of Wales and Lady Diana the Archbishop of Canterbury said, "Those who are married live happily ever after the wedding day if they persevere in the real adventure which is the royal task of creating each other and creating a more loving world" (*The Prince and the Princess*, 233).

As a Family

Philosopher Jean Jacques Rousseau said, "The first thing a child should learn is how to endure. It is what he will have most need to know." Our seven daughters, all baby boomers, did learn endurance and how to survive as a minister's family. Where we lived helped. The large, old, Victorian parsonage was a block removed from the church. On one side were woods, on the other side the grade school they attended. The house with four bedrooms offered areas of privacy. The girls were allowed to decorate their space. One painted red footprints on the ceiling. Our home was our sanctuary. Living in one home and town for forty years was a stabilizing influence.

Les's Irish sense of humor was contagious. He said he lived in a nylon jungle. Laughter abounded. On one birthday a seven-year-old gave her five-year-old sister this note, "For your birthday I give you the twenty-five cents you owe me." Another daughter, six years old, who was learning to play the piano, wrote this note to her dad: "Miss H. called that she could not play the piano at prayer meeting tonight. I'll play. Pick easy pieces."

When the oldest daughter returned from her first term of college, the youngest greeted her at the door, "We have another shower." The oldest was excited. (Seven girls and one-and-a-half baths was a challenge.) "Where?" The youngest led her to the living room where water from the bathroom above was dripping into a pail.

My daughters nicknamed me, "Mother General." On Saturdays I assigned them jobs. As soon as one job was finished, I gave new orders. One day they came as a group. "We are sick and tired of having our Saturdays spoiled with work. We have formulated a constitution." It was designed to minimize quarreling and to maximize efficiency. This document addressed important issues like who would do which chores, the penalty for failure to fulfill responsibility, a policy for borrowing from each other, who would control the hot water tap when taking joint baths, who would answer the telephone, and who would select the permissible TV programs. Anyone disobeying the constitution was set straight by her sisters. Years later, in a sociology class at Wheaton College, one of our daughters was asked by the professor to describe the features of this constitution.

Somewhere I picked up the word, "Eskimo." I used it in place of "Shut up." If the girls made too much noise when guests were present, I would call upstairs, "Eskimo." If things did not quiet down, I would raise my voice level and say, "Eskimo X." That meant that as soon as the company leaves, "I am going to discipline you."

One missionary said, "Your church doesn't have spiritual indigestion. I can feel the love there." The church people were generous in their love to us. One deacon prayed for our family at every Wednesday evening prayer meeting. People gave us hand-me-downs. A mother and daughter mended our clothes. Two ladies cut the girls' hair. One day I came home and found a daughter crying. "Mrs. B. cut my hair and it didn't need it because Mrs. S. cut it last week."

Every Christmas a deacon gave us a tree. After his death his daughter kept up the tradition. One member, a cook in an orphanage, brought us leftover turkey carcasses to make soup, canned food, and bakery items. One day, while I was out, he left bread on the porch. The girls kept their favorite brands, and took the rest to the porch of the Christian Ed director. Back home they phoned him with disguised voice, "You are the lucky recipient of a prize. Look on the front porch for your gift."

One of the trustees appointed himself as our handyman. His devices, like a coat-hanger holding up a plastic pipe, were unique. Once, when the girls were doing one of their frequent room changes and wanted to get rid of some furniture, the double bed mattress and spring got stuck in the staircase. At that moment their father walked in, half the family upstairs, and half down, trying to budge the items. He went to the phone, called the handyman who promptly came. "Kick the mattress," he said, and down it plunged.

People outside the church circles were kind to us. Our family physician, eye-doctor, and dentist gave us discounts, and our orthodontist allowed us to pay on time. In the early years we had no health insurance, so when I had a miscarriage, the surgeon let me pay in installments. The appliance store permitted us to pay, "Three months—no interest."

Building self-esteem helped survival. Family psychologist, John Rosemond, said in an interview in the *Honolulu Advertiser* (January 24, 1991, 82) that self-esteem cannot come by constantly praising children or keeping them happy. "I redefine self-esteem as self-competence. It is the discovery on the part of the child that despite his anxieties and fears he's capable of standing on his own two feet, he's capable of dealing adequately with the challenge of life. And that step-by-step discovery is what we mean by self-esteem."

Finding paying jobs helped our daughters build their self-esteem. They worked in the library, in stores, janitored in the school, baby-sat, cleaned houses and spent summers working at summer camps.

Les prevented the invasion of our family privacy by never referring to us in his sermons. The congregation found difficulty distinguishing among the girls, so they did not know which Flynn cartwheeled down the church steps.

Though it meant extra cleaning, or giving up their beds, the girls thrived on company. Who else had college presidents telling them jokes, or magazine editors discussing future articles, or musicians who practiced before their concerts? The family member "in charge of the bathroom" was pleased when one seminary president, staying with us for a weekend, said, "I'll shower at the YMCA." Missionaries gave the girls gifts and told them stories. Their favorite was an evangelist who was a magician. They enjoyed the privilege of carrying a ventriloquist's props "because he's staying at our house." Unexpected company demanded immediate action:

"clean all the junk out of the hall." "Check the bathroom." "Make coffee." "No, you can't wear your roller skates clearing the table." It meant smaller portions of meat, but also dessert which mother had hidden away.

Les gave the family Mondays. We played games, went to the candy store, or drove to a shopping mall fifteen miles away. In the summer it was a day at the beach. Vacations were spent with grandparents unless a Bible conference asked Les to speak, and innocently said, "Bring the family." On one trip to Wheaton, Illinois, a daughter said, "I feel funny." I looked at her—she had the mumps. Picture seven girls, their parents and suitcases all piled in a station wagon for a thousand-mile trip.

The church had an active youth program. The girls were involved in plays, choir, youth orchestra. All of them earned a week at camp by memorizing Bible verses. TV was carefully monitored.

The girls played tricks on each other, instead of on other children. "You never get bored at the parsonage," one neighbor said. Someone was always ready for a monopoly game. The girls traded toys, books, and clothes among themselves.

One family rule said, "You can carp at anyone at home, but do not discuss family faults with outsiders." The girls had a spirit of comradeship and family attachments. They put on skits and built a clubhouse in the woods. They all took piano lessons, and four took violin. They learned to think logically because of the philosophical discussions at the dinner table.

Singer Mahalia Jackson said, "It's easy to be independent when you've got money. But to be independent when you haven't got a thing, that's the Lord's test." The girls learned to get along on little, cutting each others' hair, repairing their own clothes, and when wanting extra things, getting a job to pay for them.

The family philosophy seemed to be that if something is worth doing, it's worth doing well; if you can't say something nice, don't say anything at all; do unto others as you would have them do unto you; be independent and unique; everything has a purpose, even if you can't know it now.

When we arrived in Nanuet, we had an eighteen-month-old girl, and I was six weeks away from having our second child. The senior deacon, his wife, and nine-year-old daughter, Peggy, paid us a visit. I invited Peggy to return after the birth of the baby. She attended school next to the parsonage, so began to come after school to play with the children. She turned out to be my answer to sanity. As she grew older, she became our baby-sitter, even going on some vacations with us. Each girl received a special birthday celebration, planned and carried out by Peggy.

Christmas was Peggy's favorite time when she lavished on them the very gifts they requested. The trips the church gave us would not have been possible without her help. One of our girls said, "Our schoolmates had their trips to Bermuda on spring vacation, but we had Peggy and her yellow convertible all year." Peggy became supervisor in a hospital for emotionally disturbed children. Her gentle, Christian caring, and disciplined life, rubbed off on our girls. Many other members of the congregation influenced their lives as well. Longtime relationships with loving, praying people gave stability and strength.

As a Person

Forty years in the same church, in the same parsonage, with the same man, plus the invasion of seven other women, made for a whirlwind existence. My background helped make my personal survival possible. My immigrant parents taught their two sons and daughter the value of work and play. They owned a business in Wheaton, Illinois, twenty-five miles west of Chicago. When things became stressful, "the boss," as my brothers called my father, would go to Chicago for the day. One evening my father heard me crying in my bedroom, and asked my problem. "I am overwhelmed," I answered. "I have a radio program to write. I'm involved in a play at church. My friends say I am neglecting them. It's too much."

My father gently said, "Bernice, pity is no solution. What you need is a change of pace. Take a day home in bed. Forget everything. Things will look brighter after you get some needed rest. No one can take better care of yourself than you." It was advice I often followed when overstressed.

A neighbor, a martyr for her family, did everything for them, and spent nothing on herself. The children grew up. They left. Her husband looked at her. He left. Seeing this tragedy taught me to spend time and money on personal appearance and intellectual pursuits. When new to the church, I was standing by my husband at the back of the church. A lady looked me up and down and said, "You have a new coat." I was taken aback. She added, "We like our minister's wife to look nice."

To enlarge my world I joined the PTA and the Historical Society. Friends I made invited me to the opera and museums in New York City. They seeded my interest in antiques.

My husband was strong on encouraging others to lead. "You can act as an adviser," he told me, "but don't take any office in church." As needs arose, I taught all classes from the nursery to the adult department. My aim was to work myself out of each job. As other people showed gifts in the areas I served, including audio-visual, historical archives, and missionary coordinator I gave them the positions. Doors opened for me to speak at women's retreats and banquets. When an invitation came, and there was no conflict, I assumed the Lord wanted me to accept.

I tried not to neglect the church. I attended all Sunday services, prayer meeting, ladies' meetings, and visited the sick and shut-in.

The Lord provided a prayer partner. I could share all and any requests with her. I was assured they would not go on the phone but to the throne. The church family proved to be loving caretakers. They gave me baby showers. When I fell down the cellar steps, injured my back, and was confined by the doctor to my bed for several weeks, one friend rearranged the bedroom. Faithful Peggy brought in hot meals. Visitors came with books, flowers and cards.

I had a living example of Christianity in action when I saw the faithfulness and diligence of Sunday school teachers, and of those who sponsored youth groups as they imprinted Christ on other lives. Home from law school, a daughter wanted to go to Sunday school. I listed the adult courses she could attend. "No, I'm going to Mrs. W's class." (Mrs. W had taught the five-year-olds over thirty years.) "I learned so much from her." This daughter now teaches the same age group in her church.

In a congregation, as in a family, certain members need you more at particular points in their journeys. I wondered if it was fair spending more time with these members. The thought came to me that Christ gave more time to certain followers in needy situations.

I wanted to be a good minister's wife, but not be suffocated by it. The church family allowed me to continually reserve the right to be myself. When the girls were small, I taught a course at a Christian college. As Family Editor of *Christian Life* magazine for ten years, I could work at home. After completing a graduate course on reading, a unique job opened in the public school which I could do on my own time schedule. After the death of our eighth daughter, a Down Syndrome baby who lived only one hour, I became a substitute teacher in the county's special education program, and taught for ten years. One of my most satisfying experiences was serving on the Board of the Conservative Baptist Foreign Mission Society for six years, which involved a seven-week trip to Africa to visit mission fields.

Before going to bed, I organized in writing the next day's duties. In addition to the must-do's, I penned in some which-to-do's. These included making someone else happy, a task I disliked doing, and a selfish wish. When the children were small, I didn't take time to exercise, but as they left the nest, I joined a health club and now go with a friend three mornings a week. Frequent visits to the library kept me up to date on magazines and books. I regularly read the *Book of Common Prayer*. A friend encouraged me to read the Bible through in a year, which I have now done for years. To help me pray I used a gimmick involving my hand. The thumb nearest to the body is for loved ones nearest me. The pointer finger is for those who point people to God. The middle, highest finger, for those who are over us in authority. The fourth finger is the weak finger, reminding me to pray for the indigenous, homeless and sick. The small finger is for my own needs.

At some time all of us go through a Gethsemane as did Jesus the night before He died. Just as God sent an angel to strengthen Him in the garden, so when I entertain demons of doubt, discouragement and disappointment, my ever-present, all-knowing, all-powerful heavenly Father sends me an angel of hope. The faithfulness of God was and is my survival. No matter what bursts my world, nothing can separate me from Him. As I look back on the things I worried about, I see the futility. Two of our daughters were expecting babies. One concerned me deeply. She had been paralyzed as a child. I had no worry about the other, but when her baby was born, it developed a serious medical problem. Christopher, our first grandchild, after surviving three operations, died at six weeks. But the other daughter experienced no problems, and recently gave birth to her sixth child. It does not pay to worry. What you worry about seldom happens—it's what you don't expect!

When Les retired, the church gave us a gala dinner, generous cash gift, silver tray, forty red long-stemmed roses, and a once-in-a-lifetime friendship quilt. Secretly the ladies sent a seven-inch square of fabric to missionaries and friends, asking each to design "a unique expression of love." They were also asked to write a short note to me on an enclosed card. They put 196 squares together as a quilt. Many of my friends were unable to share in the project, but their names and deeds are engraved on my heart.

Having both short and long term goals, and a belief in what we were doing, as a couple, as a family, and as individuals, made our ministry a serendipity survival.

11

Cultivate a Loving Congregation

How does a pastor survive forty years in the same church?

By the grace of God and the support of a loving congregation!

The congregation at Nanuet began showing care before I arrived. When called to be their pastor, we did not have a car. The Pennsylvania church I had served for four-and-a-half years had started me at $1500 a year, then raised it to $1800, an increase that did not let me buy a car. So a couple in Nanuet drove to Pennsylvania and transported my wife, my eighteen-month old daughter, and myself in their Packard to our new location.

I soon discovered I could never hope to perform my pastoral duties without a car. In my Pennsylvania pastorate, with houses built close together and next to the sidewalk, most of my congregation was within walking distance, and the main hospital a ten-minute bus ride. But not so Nanuet. My parishioners were spread over several miles; six main hospitals were located up to fifteen miles away; and nursing homes were scattered around the county. It took most of one afternoon, my first week there, to walk one mile to the end of town to express my sympathy to a man whose brother had just passed away, and then walk back to church.

So, I bought a car. Even then with a salary of $3,000 a year, how would I manage the high monthly payments? Every week for the next year, an envelope containing $5 was handed us by the church treasurer, marked "car payment" but with no name. We were told only that the gift came from two families. To this day we do not know the identity of the donors.

Another problem. Though I (and the finance company) then

owned a car, I did not know how to drive. My parents never had a car. In school most of my life, I had never learned. A young man in the congregation taught me, now 30, how to drive. Within six weeks of my arrival I passed my driver's test, just in time to drive my wife to the hospital to have our second daughter, an excellent place to be driving, given my inexperience.

These early kindnesses were the beginning of a series of gracious acts that would follow us through all the years right to our retirement. How graciously the members of the congregation accepted the arrival of the many babies who soon followed. In quick succession during the next dozen years, our third, fourth, fifth, sixth, seventh, and eighth little girls were born. As my wife has already mentioned, the eighth, a Down Syndrome baby, lived less than an hour. But prior to every birth the ladies of the church had a shower with a generous gift. Some churches would have been critical of a pastor having such a large family. But we felt the love of a congregation which opened its arms to welcome each new little life. In fact, many seemed to enjoy referring to the "the girls' dormitory," or to "Father Flinnigan of Girlstown."

Countless favors were bestowed on us. Every Christmas for forty years, a family brought us a Christmas tree. A nine-year-old girl, who came after school to see the new baby, kept coming for years, became a nurse, then a supervisor in a children's psychiatric hospital. She became a second mother to our girls, taking care of them when my wife and I went on trips, and celebrating their birthdays in a special way. She made their Christmases special by lavishing on them many lovely gifts. She served on the search committee which selected my successor.

Another family, florists, provided a beautiful arrangement for the church every Sunday, sent lovely bouquets on my wife's birthday, our wedding anniversary, and furnished flowers for all seven of our daughters' weddings. The church celebrated our twenty-fifth wedding anniversary with an after-church social and gift. After my wallet was stolen in a mugging, a member casually asked how much money I had been carrying. To my surprise, a week later I was given an envelope with bills that exceeded my loss.

At a Wednesday evening midweek meeting one of my officials thought I looked quite pale, so sent my wife and me on a vacation to Washington, D.C. (After that I often toyed with the idea of putting powder on my face before meetings.) Several members paid my way to the Congress on Evangelism in Minneapolis in 1967.

One of the repeated, thoughtful acts of the church was to remember the anniversary of our coming to Nanuet every five years. On our fifteenth anniversary they gave us a three-week trip to the Holy Land, including Portugal, Rome, Athens, and London. On our twentieth, they gave us a five-week trip around the world to visit our missionaries, with stops in Hawaii, Japan, the Philippines, Taiwan, Hong Kong, India, West Pakistan, Babylon in Iraq, Ephesus in Turkey, Switzerland, and France. On our twenty-fifth, they gave us a three-week trip to loaf in Europe with stays in Rome, Florence, Venice, Switzerland, Munich, Salzburg, Vienna, Copenhagen, and Stockholm. I always looked to make sure our documents included a return stub, not just a one-way ticket to outer Siberia! These trips served as sabbaticals, and were both educational and refreshing.

On our thirtieth, thirty-fifth, and fortieth anniversaries, travel had become quite expensive, so we were given dinners and generous cash gifts. However, in our thirty-seventh year we were able to take a seven-week trip across Africa. My wife, six years on the national board of the Conservative Baptist Foreign Mission Society, was named Africa field chairperson the final three years of her term. Her way was paid by CBFMS, while much of mine came through the help of church people. This journey took us to Senegal, Cote d'Ivoire, Kenya, Rwanda, Zaire, and Madagascar. In 46 days, we slept in 23 different places, and flew 21 times in planes from 747's to the Missionary Aviation Fellowship one-propeller model. I spoke 28 times, sometimes to missionaries, sometimes to theological students or churches through an interpreter. Counting airports, my wife and I have been in 55 in the U.S.A., and more than 70 overseas. Much of this travel was a gift from our church.

A few months before my sixty-fifth birthday the chairman and vice-chairman of our Board of Deacons called on me in my study to say, "We know you are near retirement age, but we would like you to continue as our pastor." Five years later, the year before my seventieth birthday, no such call was made. I sensed that the time to retire was approaching, but no one made any move to force me out. Now and again, a board member would ask if I had any date in view, but basically the board let me set my own timetable. So, the day before my seventieth birthday I announced my resignation, taking most folks by surprise. I set my resignation date for the end of the following February (1989), exactly forty years after my coming in February (1949).

A week before my final Sunday the church had a gala retirement-fortieth anniversary affair, showering upon us accolades, various presents, including a quilt handmade by nearly 200 women, and a generous cash gift. Because we had lived in the parsonage for 40 years, and had no equity in a home, the church voted to let us stay in the parsonage.

The continual kindness of such a caring church was a major factor in my survival through those four decades. Like marriages, some pastoral relationships are made in heaven. In certain situations the chemistry, so right between pastor and people, makes for a longtime love affair. The longer a pastor remains, the more in-depth knowledge of his parishioners he possesses. Seeing little children grow into adolescence, then marry and become parents, a pastor has suffered with them through a generation of ups-and-downs, and thereby earned their confidence. So, they more readily open up to him as a lifelong friend and family member. But for such a close-knit tie to exist, as in a marriage, both parties have to work at it.

How a Pastor Helps Build a Supportive Congregation

Regard Your People as Friends, Not as Enemies

When a pastor looks out on his Sunday congregation, he should view them as sheep, not as wolves. He should feed his sheep, care for them, and love them. Too many sermons ooze negative or judgmental overtones. Too many discourses tear down instead of building up. Sometimes pastors delight in carping criticism. On a Sunday when the attendance is low, why should a pastor scold those present because many are absent?

A hostile attitude sometimes shows through the homiletical structure of the message. Earl H. Furgeson in a chapter on "Preaching and Personality" wrote, "Here, for example, is a preacher who delivers a Thanksgiving sermon based on the healing of the ten lepers. The sermon deals in a condemnatory and sarcastic manner with the nine lepers who did not return to give thanks, and by implication it deals with the present (and absent) members of the congregation who can be identified with nine ungrateful lepers. A hostile rebuke for the sin of ingratitude exhausts the propositional content of the homily. Now, the biblical account provides, in addition to a reference to the nine ungrateful men, an account of one man who was grateful, who found joy in expressing his gratitude, and who by his faith was made whole. Why does the preacher overlook him? Why is he charmed by the negative aspects of the account? The answer is certainly to be found in the preacher himself, and a psychotherapist might locate the cause of the preacher's choleric tempers in a large quantity of unconscious, unresolved hostility which is displaced upon other people through the medium of the sermon" (*The Minister's Own Mental Health*, 126).

Though a preacher must rebuke evil when necessary, neither should he forget the good news of deliverance. The unconscious intrusion of a pastor's hostility into his sermon does not tend to build up his people, nor his relationship with them. In his Yale Lectures on Preaching John Watson said, "It seemeth to us, when we are still young, both clever and profitable to make a hearer ashamed of his sin by putting him in the pillory and pelting him with epithets. . . . As we grow older and see more of life it seems easier to put a man out of conceit with his sin by showing him the winsome and perfect form of goodness. . . . He that scolds in the pulpit, or rails, only irritates; he that appreciates and persuades wins the day" (*The Cure of Souls*, 57-58).

A pastor should avoid hurting sheep needlessly. One Sunday my sermon had a minor reference to suicide, which, though relevant, was not necessary to the main thrust of the message. I noticed a Christian couple enter. They did not come often, but I had been told that recently the body of their grown son, a suicide, had been found decomposed in a field. Out of respect for their feelings, I omitted my minor reference to suicide. I would find another time and place to help them handle their grief.

Treat Everyone Alike

A pastor should not play favorites. Some ministers have been known to lavish more attention on close friends than on other members. Naturally, a pastor needs friends whose company provides fellowship, strength and wisdom, especially in times of stress and misunderstanding. But pastoral ministry must be available to all, rich or poor, educated or uneducated, young or old, well-known or considered insignificant. Leaders should never forget James' rebuke to those who gave the best seats in church to the rich, well-dressed, and jeweled visitor, while shunting the poor, ragged, unadorned newcomer to an out-of-the-way spot. No pastor should be guilty of favoritism or discrimination.

I never wanted to know who our generous givers were, lest I unconsciously bow to their wishes. So I never knew who gave what. Our treasurer and financial secretary were tight-lipped men of impeccable integrity who never revealed confidences, or the names of donors. A few times our treasurer said, "We had a special gift of $10,000, but the giver doesn't want his identity known." And he kept the name a secret. Too many pastors have had to shade their conviction, or deal leniently with some recalcitrant, because he didn't want to offend a moneyed member.

When the pastor recognizes from the pulpit those who have done some special service for the church, he must be careful not to single out a few and omit others. What about those who work faithfully, week in and week out, in unglamorous roles, many behind the scenes? We should be sure we haven't missed someone, and that we are applying the same criteria equally to all. A pastor may be wise to appoint a committee to select those to be recognized, so responsibility for oversights do not fall on him.

Make Few Demands on Your Congregation

I belonged to the school of preachers who asked for very little. I never asked for a raise. Once in the early years, I turned down a raise, but never in later years when we had several on staff. I didn't want to jeopardize their salaries which increased the same percent as mine.

My wife and I asked very little for the parsonage. Though it was church property, we spent thousands to have the inside decorated. My wife made the parsonage a lovely and comfortable home. However, the outside was somewhat neglected, perhaps showing that churches are not always the best landlords. How thankful we were for the men from the church who spent many evening hours making needed repairs in the parsonage. Thoughtfully, they made major improvements in the parsonage when we retired.

The church never sent me to our annual meetings till after I had been pastor for more than thirty years. Not till my Associate Pastor pointed out to our board that many smaller churches paid their pastors' way to annual conventions did our church place this expense in our annual budget.

I did ask for two items in late years. One had to do with Social Security, which I had fully paid myself without any help from the church. But when our staff grew, every member had half his or her Social Security paid by the church. When I pointed this out to the board, they graciously made a generous adjustment. On my thirtieth anniversary the board increased my vacation to five weeks a year.

On my thirty-fifth, I asked for and was granted six weeks of vacation.

I realize that my hesitancy to make demands may jeopardize my successors. I also am aware that today fellows starting in the ministry are given in seminary a list of benefits to negotiate. Overall, I feel that my nondemanding attitude was a factor in my survival.

Encourage Members to Have Concern for Each Other

The supreme virtue is love, not only for God, but also for the brethren. Love for each other signals to the world that we are Christ's disciples. Through the years I learned of many acts of kindness quietly performed which never received public attention. Other acts became known, such as when the church sponsored a young Cambodian refugee couple with a baby, then also brought over the wife's mother and four brothers. A few of our people spent much time, energy, and money in helping these families adjust to American culture, all in the name of Christ.

One morning a stranger, a Haitian girl, with nowhere to go, came to my study to ask for help. In the church office a group of ladies were preparing the monthly mailing. Leaving the girl in my study, I slipped into the office and explained her plight to the ladies. Without hesitation one of them offered to take her to her home. As a result, the girl had a temporary home, secured a job, graduated from a local college, raised her son, now has her own place, and is an active, joyful Christian.

If we can encourage members to care for each other, those members will likely also affirm their pastor.

Never Nurse Resentment

The apostle John wrote to a church about the coming of some itinerant preachers. His letter fell into the hands of dictatorial Diotrophes, who arrogantly refused to welcome these preachers, and forbade others to receive them. Somehow succeeding in getting the majority under his thumb, he pushed himself forward to usurp authority, ousting from the church any who opposed him (3 John 9–10). Diotrophes was the archtype of vain, self-seeking, self-appointed overseers who lord it over their brethren and browbeat all who get in their way.

A member may enjoy being a big fish in a little pond. If the pond grows too big, he may move to a smaller place where he can resume his feeling of importance. But in all the commotion he may wreak havoc for pastor and people.

A neurotic can cause a lot of trouble for a pastor. Usually a feeling of loyalty restrains his hostility, but at times he may be very vindictive. Aiming his hostility at his minister, a neurotic may zero in on his target relentlessly until he either humiliates or ruins him. Such a person should be confronted in the biblical way, and if necessary, the church should remove him from a place of leadership, even excommunicating him on the grounds of divisiveness. But often a church moves too slowly or indecisively with the result that the minister is the one to leave. It is possible for a Diotrophes, or for a few cantankerous people, to undercut longevity.

But in any case, a pastor should not harbor resentment or seek revenge. Holding a grudge carries a high price tag, causing stomach upset, fatigue, insomnia, even ulcers. Sometimes someone says with clenched teeth, "I'll get even with him if it's the last thing I ever do!" Often it *is* the last thing he ever does.

How a Congregation Helps a Pastor Survive

A caring pastor helps build a loving church, and in turn, a loving church helps a pastor survive. Here are ways a supportive church can help its pastor to stay, and to stay happy.

Pay Your Pastor Adequately

To some, paying the preacher may seem like a mundane matter, but it is a scriptural principle. The Bible says that the laborer is worthy of his wages. Paul wrote, "Anyone who receives instruction in the word must share all good things with his instructor" (Gal. 6:6 NIV). Too many congregations have this attitude, "Lord, You keep him humble, and we'll keep him poor."

Incidentally, since the twelve tribes of Israel each brought a tenth to the ministering Levites, the income of the Levites averaged twelve tenths of the other tribes. Old Testament clergy received twenty percent higher salary than their congregation, a situation likely the reverse of most ministers' wages today.

When a minister receives a raise, congregations have little idea how much that act of appreciation stimulates his dedication.

Protect Your Pastor

Protect his *time*. A phone is a pastor's stock-in-trade, and he expects to get phone calls. But don't take up his time with irrelevant, unimportant matters.

Don't expect him to show up for every committee meeting. Find out where you can put your spiritual gifts to use, and release your pastor for the tasks to which he has been called.

Protect his *reputation*. Don't criticize him carelessly, nor before others. Don't serve roast preacher for Sunday dinner.

The church in which I was reared suffered much dissension. Its pastors experienced trouble. But I never knew about any of it till I became a Christian at age fifteen, joined the church, and learned what went on inside. My parents never talked about church troubles in front of me at home. Had they done so, perhaps I would never have entered the ministry. Some parents openly criticize their pastor over the dinner table and then wonder why their children won't listen to his preaching. You cannot build up the Lord's work while tearing down its workers.

Protect his *mistakes*. A pastor is human and will make mistakes. I had a holy horror through the years of forgetting a funeral engagement, or wedding. To my knowledge my fear was never realized, except for one possible incident. A wedding rehearsal was scheduled for a Friday evening. But the couple came Thursday night, and when I didn't show and couldn't be reached, they held the rehearsal without me. The wedding went with such precision that I pondered the possibility of missing all rehearsals! The bride claims she told me of the change going out the door the previous Sunday, but I had no recollection of any such conversation. The bride was not offended in any way, laughed it off, and never mentioned it again.

Longtime pastorates have congregations who accept their ministers as human beings, allow room for mistakes, and have the ability and stamina to work through problems. Instead of wanting to fire the pastor, the people adopt a nonaccusatory approach, "Let's solve the issue. Somehow we'll work it out."

Protect his *position*. One church officer remarked to me, "I'm amazed at the rude way people rebuke our pastor. They seem to have little regard for his office." Paul wrote, "Respect those who work hard among you, who are over you in the Lord and who admonish you. Hold them in the highest regard in love because of their work" (1 Thess. 5:12, 13 NIV). Three times in Hebrews 13 the author calls for such respect (7, 17, 24),

How often my mother would remark, when she saw a pastor suffering mistreatment, "Who can stretch forth his hand against the Lord's anointed, and be guiltless" (1 Sam. 26:9)? She was quoting David before he became king. Hounded by King Saul who sought to kill him, in the providence of God David twice cornered Saul, was twice urged by his advisers to kill Saul and take over the throne, but twice refused to lay a finger on Saul. Old Testament king or New Testament pastor, my mother felt that no one could stretch a hand against the Lord's anointed without incurring the Lord's displeasure. When I've seen parents treating a pastor roughly, I've felt like saying, "Be careful how you handle your pastor. Some day your son may grow up and become a minister. How would you like him to get the same treatment?"

Promote Your Pastor

Talk him up. Brag about him legitimately. Tell your friends how you get so much out of his sermons. Invite them to come and hear him. Boost both him and his wife.

Support him by faithful attendance at the stated services. And by serving where you can. It's impossible for a church to operate without many willing workers. Cooperate with new ideas, even with new music that's not to your taste. Seek the unity of the church. Nothing can give a church a black eye in the community sooner than the notoriety of a church fight.

Encourage your pastor. Enough people will make snide remarks. Your supportive words will buoy his spirit. I recall one lady saying at an anniversary when I was given an overseas trip, "I suppose you'll count the time your trip takes as your vacation." How thankful I was for an official who sweetly said, "No, this is not vacation time. The church has given him this trip as a gift over and above his regular vacation period."

I always felt badly over an incident involving our Director of Christian Education. When given a free two-week tour to the Holy Land, he received permission to take the trip from our Board of Deacons who knew its educational and inspirational value. On his return the Board of Trustees, who felt that vacation time came within their jurisdiction, ruled that our Director must count that two-week trip as vacation. Though I intervened, the result was a compromise, one week to be considered vacation. I'm sure this Trustee action was a factor, conscious or subconscious, in his early acceptance of a position elsewhere.

Perhaps you can serve as ears for the pastor. Isolated in his ivory tower, he may be missing the pulse of the congregation, to which you can tip him off kindly, as a friend. One pastor told a confidant, "I received an anonymous letter criticizing my children's sermons. That's the third negative comment in less than a month on those object lessons. I've about decided to drop them." His confidant went to work. A week later he reported, "I know of only two people who dislike your children's sermons. I know at least thirty parents who think they're most profitable. I have a hunch that anonymous letter came from one of those two persons. Don't be scared off by a couple of vocal people."

I'll never forget the encouragement of two leaders when in my early years we finally reached an attendance of 100 at an Easter service. When I wondered out loud if we would ever attain that number again, these two godly men replied without hesitation, "Before long we'll have over 100 every Sunday, not just Easter." And they were right. For years we had 400 Sunday mornings. How their optimism lifted my spirits on that Easter Sunday. And of course, those three overseas trips gave us a great lift.

A century ago, R. W. Dale, respected pastor in Birmingham, England, suffered moods of depression. In such a state, walking down a street, he was greeted by a poor lady whose name he did not know, "God bless you, Dr. Dale. If you could only know how you have made me feel hundreds of times, and what a happy home you have given me—God bless you!" Dale said that the sun broke through the fog of depression so that he could breathe God's fresh air again. Encouragement is good medicine.

One way to have pastors healthy in body, mind and spirit, according to Dr. Tim Blanchard, former General Director of the Conservative Baptist Association of America, is for more church people to be like Onesiphorus. Paul said that Onesiphorus often refreshed him (2 Tim. 1:6). On one occasion he traveled over 800 miles to Rome where he diligently searched for Paul in the prisons until he found him (v. 17). Onesiphorus frequently found ways to relieve Paul of the "heat" so he could cool off and relax.

Blanchard wrote, "Have you ever provided such a relaxing respite for one of your pastors or busy ministry leaders? Arranging for a two-day mini-vacation at a nice hotel, a dinner-for-two gift certificate, tickets to a ball game, or a day alone for a couple with baby-sitting provided are some examples of what can be done" (*Conservative Baptist*, Winter 1989, 2).

Pray for Your Pastor

Privately, and in public, lift up your pastor before the throne of grace. His task is extremely difficult. He needs the intercession of his people for wisdom, grace, and strength.

A new pastor came to Calvary Baptist Church, New York City, decades ago. Before a year had elapsed, a deacon said to other board members, "He's not going to make it." But they all resolved to pray for him. He stayed over forty years. He was Dr. Stuart McArthur. A hall in that church is named after him.

Spurgeon, asked the secret of his success, replied simply, "My people pray for me."

If you want your pastor to survive, *pay, protect,* and *promote* him. But above all, *pray* for him.

12

Don't Blow It When You're on Top

In the summer of 1989 Pete Rose, baseball's leading all-time hitter with twenty-six years in uniform, and seemingly destined for the Hall of Fame, was barred from baseball and later sentenced to prison. The baseball commissioner ruled, "The banishment for life of Pete Rose from baseball is the sad end of a sorry episode. One of the game's greatest players has engaged in a variety of acts which have stained the game, and he must now live with the consequences of those acts."

How often we read of some eminent person suddenly taking a shameful tumble. As the adage puts it, "There's no fool like an old fool." A judge who had presided over a New York City court for decades was recently found guilty of a crime and led out of that very same court in handcuffs, destined for jail.

Christian leaders at the height of their career have suffered similar ignominy, like Jim Bakker. During Bakker's trial in a North Carolina court a newspaper executive in Virginia wrote a letter to a magazine, saying he preferred to remember Jim and Tammy from the days when they didn't live high on the hog as famous TV preachers. He told of a rally sponsored by local businessmen with limited finances who had invited Paul Harvey as speaker. With very few tickets sold these men came in panic to the newspaper executive to beg for free news space. It occurred to the newsman, whose kids loved watching Jim and Tammy's puppet show on cable TV, that an event drawing children would bring parents too. With trepidation he phoned Jim Bakker who told him that he would come gratis. Thousands of children came to the rally. All Jim and

Tammy received was 75 cents to pay a bridge toll and $10 for gas. The newsman ended his letter, "The other day when I saw Jim Bakker a broken man and manacled in the hands of U.S. marshals, I could only cry" (*Charisma*, November 1989).

From lowly beginnings and with the best of intentions many godly people rise to places of leadership, then blow it. Former PTL Vice President Richard Dortch, sentenced to eight years in prison, lamented in court, "I failed my Master, my family, and myself. I lost the thing that I lived for—my ministry."

BE VIGILANT

To survive, caution must be exercised to the very end. The apostle Paul, realizing the need for constant vigilance, wrote, "I run straight to the goal with purpose in every step. I fight to win. I'm not just shadowboxing or playing around. Like an athlete I punish my body, treating it roughly, training it to do what it should, not what it wants to. Otherwise I fear that after enlisting others for the race, I myself might be declared unfit and ordered to stand aside" (1 Cor. 9:26, 27 TLB).

The Old Testament contains many stories of leaders, who in later life were tripped up by pride or lust. A. W. Pink commented, "It is striking to observe that Scripture records not a single instance of a young saint disgracing his profession. Recall the histories of young Joseph; the Hebrew maid in Naaman's household; David as a stripling engaging Goliath; Daniel's early days and his three youthful companions in the furnace; and it will be found that all of them quitted themselves nobly. On the other hand, there are numerous examples where men in middle life and of gray hairs grievously dishonored their Lord." He added that young Christians sense their frailty, but "some older Christians seem far less conscious of their danger, and so God often suffers them to have a fall, that He may stain the pride of their self-glory, and that others may see it is nothing in the flesh—standing, rank, age, or attainments—which insures our safety, but that He upholds the humble and casts down the proud" (*Exposition of Hebrews*, 957).

Toward the end of the wilderness journey, Moses rebelled against the commandment of God and was not allowed to enter the promised land (Num. 20:7–12). When anointed king at the start of his career, Saul remarked, "Am I not a Benjaminite, of the smallest of the tribes of Israel?" (1 Sam. 9:21). But after many victories, the humble king grew haughty, flagrantly and repeatedly disobeyed God, evoking at his death this exclamation, "How are the mighty fallen!" (2 Sam. 1:9). David fell into the sins of adultery and murder after he had become a powerful king.

Solomon, who at first reigned with great wisdom and glory, loved many forbidden, foreign women. But "as Solomon grew old, his wives turned his heart after other gods, and his heart was not fully devoted to the Lord his God" (1 Kings 11:4 NIV). Because of this the Lord divided his kingdom.

After Rehoboam, who succeeded Solomon, had established his position as king, "and he had become strong, he and all Israel with him abandoned the law of the Lord" (2 Chron. 12:1 NIV).

For King Uzziah successes came rapidly. Jerusalem's walls were strengthened. Military outposts were established. Cisterns were built for rain storage. Prosperity, unparalleled since Solomon's time, prevailed. Intoxicated with power, Uzziah lifted his heart in pride. Usurping priestly function, he pressed into the holy place, a censer in hand. But before the usurper could scatter incense, spots of leprosy appeared on his forehead. Shoved out by the priests, he remained a victim of leprosy for life, living in enforced isolation and removed from government work (2 Chron. 26:16–21).

When Sennacherib, king of Assyria, tried to terrify the defenders of Jerusalem with his pompous boast of power and supremacy, the Lord warned him through Isaiah, "Because your rage against me and your insolence has reached my ears, I will put my hook in your nose and my bit in your mouth, and I will make you return by the way you came" (2 Kings 19:28 RSV). The angel of the Lord destroyed the entire Assyrian army in one night. Soon after, Sennacherib was slain by his sons.

Hezekiah, the godly king of Judah, whom the Lord rescued from the threat of boastful Sennacherib's invasion, became immensely respected by the surrounding nations. About this time Hezekiah, becoming critically ill, prayed to the Lord Who replied with a miracle. However, says the record, "Hezekiah didn't respond with true thanksgiving and praise, for he had become proud" (2 Chron. 32:25 TLB). Though Hezekiah then humbled himself, he again displayed pride by imprudently showing his treasures to some Babylonian messengers. Isaiah then prophesied that the day would come when all those treasures, plus all of Hezekiah's possessions, would be carried away into Babylon.

Walking on his palace roof, King Nebuchadnezzar became enamored of his accomplishments. Had he not conquered the known world? Surveying the city below, he boasted with arrogant egocentricity, "Is not this great Babylon I have built . . . by my mighty power and for the glory of my majesty?" (Dan. 4:30 NIV). With the words still on his lips, a voice from heaven told him that his kingdom had departed from him, and that he would behave like an animal. Nebuchadnezzar's hair grew as long as eagles' feathers, and his nails like the claws of a bird. Scholars believe he suffered the animallike psychosis, lycanthropy.

These Old Testament stories were written to warn us against similar pitfalls. Leaders should guard against making a fool of themselves after success in ministry. Someone put it, "Let another's shipwreck be your beacon." In his *Focus on the Family* newsletter (October 1989), James Dobson tells of walking up and down the rows of booths at the Booksellers Convention at Atlantic City in 1976, where he was to be the banquet speaker on the final evening. Seeing his books displayed in several places, and a large photograph of himself prominently positioned, he sensed the Lord saying to him, "Jim, you can see that I have chosen to make you visible and influential among My people for purposes that you may not comprehend. In so doing, I am making My church vulnerable to you. You will be able to hurt and disappoint the family of believers by the things you do and say. Don't mess it up! Bridle your tongue. Guard your behavior. Raise your ethical standard. Protect My people!"

The next year Dobson launched Focus on the Family, and two years later his first film series which made his ministry known nationwide. Then added Dobson in his newsletter, "Now, more than 13 years later, the warning I received in Atlantic City still rings in my ears. My greatest fear is that my inadequacies and imperfections will lead me to do something to hurt the cause of Christ. It could happen so easily, despite my determination to avoid a major blunder. When one becomes very visible in the Christian community, especially in today's environment, every step can be on a land mine. I'm not talking about the kind of evil that devastated other large ministries in the past two years. I have no intention of committing deliberate and blatant misconduct. But there are other insidious dangers lurking in the shadows, such as a major financial mistake, or an on-air blunder, or the media distortions of a Bundy-like episode, or even a lawsuit in this litigious society. I am keenly aware that Satan hates this ministry, and he will do anything he can—not only to bring it down, but to discredit the Kingdom in the process."

Dr. Charles E. Blair, pastor of Calvary Temple in Denver, confesses to the hazards of success in his book, *The Man Who Could Do*

No Wrong. His 2,300-capacity auditorium often overflowed at all three Sunday services. The blurb on the back cover reads, "He grew up on the wrong side of the tracks. He built one of the largest churches in America. Then he made a mistake." One day the newspapers carried the humiliating headline, "Blair indicted: Pastor, Fund-raiser Accused of Fraud." Charged with 21 fraudulent practices in the sale of church securities, he faced the possibility of a $100,000 fine, plus up to 60 years in the penitentiary.

When Blair was fingerprinted, the clerk, placing one of the minister's hands in the ink, said, "Twenty years ago I was driving my car, listening to your radio show, Dr. Blair. I pulled over to the side of the road and surrendered my life to Jesus. I never dreamed I'd be taking the fingerprints of the same preacher."

Found guilty, Blair was fined $12,750.00 and placed on five years' probation. Still pastor of this thriving church, Blair outlines lessons he learned and suggests ways to avoid ego trips. To his great credit he aims to pay in full all who hold bonds. The foreword speaks of "success beyond his wildest dreams to public humiliation" (John and Elizabeth Sherrill, Chosen Books).

J. B. Phillips began his well-known translation of the New Testament to encourage his bomb-threatened London congregation. From this humble beginning he launched into a snowballing career of writing, radio broadcasting, and lecturing. Though he enjoyed success, its cost was high. In his autobiography, *The Price of Success*, Phillips wrote, "I was tasting the sweets of success to an almost unimaginable degree. My health was excellent; my future prospects were rosier than my wildest dreams could ever suggest; applause, honor, and appreciation met me wherever I went. . . . I was not aware of the dangers of success. The subtle corrosion of character, the unconscious changing of values, and the secret monstrous growth of a vastly inflated idea of myself seeped slowly into me. Vaguely, I was aware of this, and like some frightful parody of St. Augustine, I prayed, 'Lord, make me humble—but not yet.' I can still savour the sweet and gorgeous taste of it all. . . . But it is very plain to me now why my one-man kingdom of power and glory had to stop." Phillips describes how his euphoria of success was followed by his plunge into years of deep depression, and yet how in the end victory prevailed (8).

J. Oswald Sanders observed that the "very fact that a man has risen to a position of leadership and prominence tends to engender a secret self-congratulation and pride which, if not checked, will unfit him for further advancement in the service of the kingdom"

(*Pulpit Helps*, December 1989, 1). Sanders explained that popularity might go to a leader's head, tempting him into compromising practices in order to hang on to his high and mighty seat and to enjoy the spoils thereof. He might be tempted to forget that it's the Lord Who is responsible for his elevation and Who could easily transfer his honors to another.

The leader who tastes success may come to believe in his own infallibility. Because God is blessing him, the leader assumes that his assessment of situations must be correct, making him unwilling to concede the possibility of mistakes in judgment. Moreover, he somehow feels he is above the law, so that whatever he does is right. Such conceit results in carelessness. Before he realizes it, the overconfident leader is guilty of some stupid indiscretion. No wonder the warning, "Wherefore let him that thinketh he standeth take heed lest he fall" (1 Cor. 10:12).

Today's Christian public often treats successful writers, singers, and TV preachers as superstars. Writing in *Eternity* magazine, Joseph Bayly warned that "the eminently successful Christian may begin to believe the publicity that's written about him/her (and) may come to have a bloated opinion of his importance as a result of being interviewed, having his picture on magazine covers, being adulated by a fan club that hangs on his every word and accepts his every action" (Sept. 1985, 88).

A pastor should be the first to recognize that any seeming success comes from the Lord. When all goes well—increasing crowds, growing budgets, building programs, souls won and edified—a mature leader knows where the credit should go. Robert Murray McCheyne, returning home from a service on which divine blessing had unmistakably rested, used to kneel down and symbolically place a crown of success on the brow of the Lord, Who said, "My glory will I not give to another" (Isa. 42:8).

Samuel Chadwick summed it up well, "If successful, don't crow; if defeated, don't croak."

RESIST TEMPTATION AT THE START

No leader falls suddenly. A pastor's fall from grace may surprise an unsuspecting congregation, but his public indiscretion has been preceded by an inner landslide. Wrongful deeds begin as inordinate thoughts. A burglar cases a bank, devises a plan, then holds up the bank. Every kidnapping was once an idea. Every extramarital affair was first a fantasy. Achan confessed, "When I saw among the spoils a goodly Babylonish garment, and two hundred shekels of silver, and a wedge of gold of fifty shekels weight, then I coveted them, and took them" (Josh. 7:21). From the vantage of his palace roof King David gazed at a "woman washing herself" (2 Sam. 11:2).

Since temptation starts in the imagination, that's where to get the victory. The best way to break up a forward pass is by sacking the quarterback. If a team can keep a hitter from getting to first base, he'll never score. If a person can nip a temptation in the bud, he'll never succumb.

Jay Adams calls getting the victory at the beginning, "resistance." Because man possesses a brain, he is able to delay his response to a temptation and choose an alternate course of action. But even if a person fails to resist temptation in its initial state, he still need not let it run its full course into an act of evil. He has the Holy Spirit and the Word to help him break the chain of sin. Though it is possible through restraint to curtail the process of evil along its course, the preferable alternative is to resist evil before it gets going (*The Christian Counselor's Manual*, 197).

A well-known maxim says, "Sow a thought; reap an act. Sow an act; reap a habit. Sow a habit; reap a character. Sow a character; reap a destiny." Since there's destiny (and survival) in thought, we should guard our thoughts. No Christian, leader or layperson, should flirt with temptation. A proverb says, "When you're looking at your neighbor's melon patch, you can't keep your mouth from watering, but you can run." Another puts it, "He who would not enter the room of sin must not sit by the door of temptation."

A leader should not entertain a temptation. A mind is a reception room for all kinds of thoughts—good, bad, and indifferent. Whatever thoughts are welcomed inside this room will ultimately determine character and conduct.

> *It's not what we think we are,*
> *but what we think, we are.*

A passing impure thought, unwelcomed, is not sinful. So do not dally with temptation, but deny it at the very beginning. The farther down the road a person travels through X-rated films, erotic books, and filthy fantasies, the harder it will be to stop short of sin. As long as temptation is just knocking outside the door, you have not sinned. But when temptation enters and discusses with the mind, entices the affections, and debates with the heart, you have entered into temptation.

To keep from succumbing to temptation, we need to fill our minds with good thoughts. Paul, as up-to-date as any psychology text, advised, "whatever is true, whatever is noble, whatever is right, whatever is pure, whatever is lovely, whatever is admirable—if anything is excellent or praiseworthy—think about such things" (Phil. 4:8 NIV). To think such thoughts requires saturation in that Book which is so full of lofty thoughts.

Schedule a Daily Devotional Period

To make the mind a holy place instead of a horror chamber we must cultivate the inner man. Isaiah said, "They that wait upon the Lord shall renew their strength" (40:31). Victorious Christian living for preacher or parishioner does not exist apart from a period of daily private devotions. The absence of this daily exercise has been termed the number one reason for backsliding. Even our great example, the Lord Jesus Christ, repeatedly in His ministry withdrew to a private place to seek heavenly help for His earthly ministry. Whether at morning or night, we need a quiet time to refresh and restore our souls.

Daily devotion is like a timeout in a football game when a team recoups its forces for the next play. Taking time with the Lord grants opportunity for self-examination. What thoughts am I entertaining? What about my motives? What direction am I headed? The quiet hour helps us evaluate our priorities, fix new strategies, and receive strength for the battle at hand.

An editorial in *Decision* magazine posed the promise, "How to Keep One's Faith While in Seminary." It pictured hundreds of young men coming home for Christmas after their first semester in a seminary, shaken by assaults, direct and indirect, on the authority of Scriptures. How can they pick up the pieces of a battered faith? The editorial ended, "There is a way through for the theologue. By putting on the whole armor of God." This spiritual armor, not seen by the naked eye, "is fashioned out of the discipline of a day-to-day diet of God's Word, and the consciousness of a personal walk with Christ" (December 1963).

Giants of the faith have stressed the inner life over outer activities. George Müller saw the danger of substituting action for meditation. To hurry to help in a public service without proper waiting on the Lord was to care more for quantity than quality of service. He said, "The primary business to which I ought to attend every day is not how much I might serve Him, but how I might have my inner man nourished." Oswald Chambers said the biggest enemy of devotion to Christ is service to Christ. Especially is this true of a leader who can become very busy, neglect his inner life, become easy prey to temptation, and make a fool of himself at the zenith of his career. Paul explained, "This is the reason that we never collapse. The outward man does indeed suffer wear and tear, but every day the inward man receives fresh strength" (2 Cor. 4:16 PHILLIPS).

Two indispensable elements of daily devotions are Bible reading and prayer. The Bereans were commended because they searched the Scriptures daily (Acts 17:11). Likened to both milk and meat, the Bible is spiritual food. Jeremiah said, "Thy words were found, and I did eat them" (15:16). George Müller, who read the Bible through over a hundred times, made this statement, "I look upon it as a lost day when I have not had a good time over the Word of God. Friends often say, 'I have so much to do, so many people to see. I cannot find time for Scripture study.' Perhaps there are not many who have more to do than I. For more than half a century I have never known one day when I had not more business than I could get through. For four years I have had annually about 30,000 letters, and most of these have passed through my own hands. Then, as pastor of a church with 1,200 believers, great has been my care. Besides, I have had charge of five immense orphanages; also, at my publishing depot, the printing and circulating of millions of tracts, books, and Bibles; but I have always made it a rule never to begin work until I have had a good season with God and his Word. The blessing I have received has been wonderful" (*Our Daily Bread*, 12/7/88).

A man testified foolishly during a Bible conference that he hoped to receive enough spiritual nourishment from the week of meetings to last him the rest of his life. Imagine expecting a lavish Sunday dinner to provide enough energy for the rest of one's life! An army that didn't eat for a few days would be too weak to fight. Does this explain why some believers are not good soldiers of the cross?

The term, "nutritional time bomb," refers to deficiencies which remain undiscovered for years and then suddenly manifest themselves in serious illness. The spiritually undernourished person (or pastor) may discover, under temptation, that his soul is too weak to weather the storm.

After the Lord has spoken to us through the Word, we are ready to speak to Him in prayer. Our prayer may reflect our response to what we just read. Perhaps, there was a command to be obeyed, a sin to be confessed, some guidance to be sought, some care to be cast on the Lord. Through prayer God draws us into fellowship with Himself. Survival requires a strong personal commitment to Jesus Christ.

MAINTAIN INTEGRITY

A pastor must practice what he preaches, else he will tear the fabric of his integrity. How dare a preacher urge his flock to tithe, and have the nerve not to tithe himself? How can a minister preach on having a daily devotional period if he does not have his own quiet time? How hollow to extol the need of witnessing for the Master, and yet rarely share the gospel with anyone. I recall how frustrated and almost hypocritical I felt one semester while teaching a course on Evangelism at Nyack College till one class I was able to report leading a man to Christ in his living room the night before.

Evaluation surveys can help keep a pastor and congregation honest. Twice through the years our morning congregation filled out questionnaires for review. One was led by the general director of our denomination, the other by an organization based in Denver, Colorado. Both showed up areas that needed attention.

To stay long in a pastorate requires integrity. A preacher with a limited supply of flashy sermons and mesmerizing gimmicks may bewitch a congregation for a few years before changing churches. But in a long pastorate, parishioners get to know if their minister practices what he preaches. If not genuine, he will soon be exposed.

Sometimes integrity can work against a pastor's survival. Because integrity requires a pastor to speak the truth in love, at times he may have to choose between the role of unpopular prophet or popular leader. Honesty may then lead to his resignation. Sad as this may be, integrity should take precedence over survival.

KEEP GROWING

It's less demanding to be the teacher of a congregation for a short pastorate than for a long term. Over the long haul a pastor may begin to exhaust his store of knowledge. So, to stay on, he will need to augment his education formally or informally. J. H. Lewis and Gordon A. Palmer in *What Every Christian Should Know* report that "In a survey of 255 pastors in nineteen denominations, one of the most significant findings was the high correlation between pastors who dropped out of ministry and who also had a narrow education (only in Bible). When the going got tough, they lacked the perspective their liberal arts-trained colleagues had that might have enabled them to stay with their call" (*Christianity Today*, 1989, 28). Maybe the reason some denominations limit a minister's stay in the same church is the fear that he will run out of gas, scrape the bottom of his sermon barrel, grow stale, and make the congregational troops restless.

No one can keep up with the proliferation of books coming off the press today. A pastor must somehow discover the books that should be read, then make time in his schedule to read them. I have always admired the fellows who could read, or browse thoroughly, three or four books a day, but I could never maintain such a schedule. Six to seven books a month was my limit.

Ministerial seminars are so numerous that a pastor could attend one almost every week of the year. This would be impossible. But a pastor should take advantage of a few practical, pertinent seminars annually. He needs to pursue some form of continuing education. How grateful I was for a ten-week course in mental illness offered by the chaplain of a nearby state hospital nearly 40 years ago. Each week a different psychiatrist explained a type of mental illness, brought in persons who suffered this particular malady, and helped us understand how to react to parishioners showing its symptoms. This gave me an entirely new approach to the many emotionally ill I would meet through the years. I also recall with pleasure the benefit of a seminar on church growth led by Dr. Peter Wagner.

Though the average pastorate today is short, new concepts relating to the minister's family life have made longer pastorates more appealing to some. For example, for a ministers' wife to work in secular employment is quite commonly accepted today. So, a pastor with a wife who likes her job will find it more difficult to leave his church. Also, more pastors are purchasing their own homes today, and they find it more comfortable to stay put than to go through the hassle of selling and house-hunting. But for whatever reason a pastor may wish to stay, he must determine to grow personally and educationally, or else become repetitive and dull. A growing pastor will experience a ministry both rewarding and meaningful.

In a world of change, how blessed are congregations that have pastors who model stability. Long-time pastorates provide a steadying influence around which parishioners may rally as their lives become grounded in Christian grace. It was somewhat sobering toward the end of my ministry to hear several say, "You are the only pastor I have ever had."

Whatever policies I have adopted, or techniques other pastors have found helpful in surviving in the ministry, we all acknowledge that unless the Lord build the house, we labor in vain who build.

Bibliography

Adams, Jay. *The Christian Counselor's Manual*, Baker, 1973, p. 197.

Allen, Mary Rebecca. "The Writing Army of CWI" in *Power*, October 10, 1954, p. 2.

Bayly, Joseph. "Out of My Mind" in *Eternity* magazine, September 1985, p. 88.

Blanchard, Tim. *Conservative Baptist* magazine, Winter 1989, p. 2.

Blizzard, Samuel W. "The Protestant Parish Minister's Integrating Role," in *The Minister's Own Mental Health*, edited by Wayne E. Oates, Channel Press, 1961, p. 126.

British Weekly. No documentation, but the substantially same item appeared in the "To Illustrate" column, titled "Preaching Effect," *Leadership*, Spring 1985, p. 68.

Churchill, Winston. *The Gathering Storm*, Houghton, 1948, p. 421.

Cornell, George W. "Firings are high among Southern Baptist pastors," Associated Press religion column in the Boca Raton *Sun-Sentinel*, February 17, 1990.

Cousins, Norman. *The Anatomy of an Illness*, W.W. Norton, 1979, p. 91.

Covert, Harry. "Letters" section in *Charisma* magazine, November 1989.

Dobson, James. *Focus on the Family* newsletter, October 1989.

Faulkner, Brooks R. *Forced Termination*, Broadman, 1986, p. 8.

Flynn, Leslie B. *Come Alive with Illustrations*, Baker, 1987.

Flynn, Leslie B. *19 Gifts of the Spirit*, Victor, 1974.

Furgeson, Earl H. "Preaching and Personality," in *The Minister's Own Mental Health*, edited by Wayne E. Oates, Channel Press, 1961, p. 126.

"How to Keep One's Faith While in Seminary," Editorial in *Decision* magazine, December 1963, p. 2. (No name on editorial, but probably written by the editor, Sherwood Wirt.)

Hunter, Joel C. "Defusing Spiritual Depth Charges" in *Leadership* magazine, Spring 1987, pp. 48-50.

King, Norman. *The Prince and the Princess*, Simon and Schuster, 1983, p. 233.

Lewis, Jo H. and Palmer, Gordon A. *What Every Christian Should Know*, Victor, 1989, p. 28.

Lloyd-Jones, D. Martyn, *Healing and the Scriptures*, Oliver Nelson, division of Thomas Nelson Publishers, 1982, p. 41.

MacLennan, David. *Resources for Sermon Preparation*, Westminster Press, Philadelphia, 1957, p. 7.

McBride, Michael G. "The Vocational Stress of Ministry," in *Ministry* magazine, January 1989, pp. 4-7.

Müller, George. *Our Daily Bread*, Radio Bible Class, Grand Rapids, MI., December 7, 1988.

New York Times. March 25, 1967.

Newsletter. "The Perfect Preacher Has Been Found," Grace U.M. Church, Davenport, Iowa.

Phillips, J.B. *The Price of Success*, Harold Shaw Publishers, 1964, p. 8.

Pink, A.W. *Exposition of Hebrews*, Baker, 1954, p. 957.

Riley, W.B. *Pastoral Problems*, Fleming H. Revell, 1936, p. 218.

Rosemond, John. *Honolulu Advertiser*, January 24, 1991, B2.

Rosen, Moishe. Personal letter dated January 3, 1965.

Sanders, J. Oswald. "The Peculiar Perils of Leadership" in *Pulpit Helps*, Chattanooga, TN, December 1989, p. 1.

Schaller, Lyle E. *Activating the Passive Church*, Abingdon, 1981, pp. 145, 146.

Schaller, Lyle E. *Survival Tactics in the Parish*, Abingdon, 1977, pp. 13, 27.

Sherrill, John and Elizabeth. *The Man Who Could Do No Wrong*, Chosen Books, 1981, back cover.

Spurgeon, C.H. *Lectures to My Students*, First Series, Marshall Brothers, pp. 23, 24, 28, 174, 175.

Stowell, Joseph M., III. "Of Shepherds and Sheep" in *Moody Alumni* magazine, Winter 1988, p. 2.

Stott, John. Interview, "Humble Scribe" in *Christianity Today*, September 8, 1989, p. 63.

Thomas, William C. *The Pastor and Church Administration*, Conservative Baptist Press, 1978, p. 18.

Vincent, Eileen. *C.T. Studd and Priscilla*, Worldwide Evangelization Crusade, 1987, pp. 223-235.

Watson, John. *The Cure of Souls* (Yale Lectures on Preaching), Dodd, Mead, & Co., 1896, pp. 57, 58.

Wells, Joel. *Coping in the Eighties*, Thomas More Press, 1986, pp. 95, 96.

Wiersbe, Warren W. and David W. *Making Sense of the Ministry*, Baker, 1969, pp. 71, 89, 106.

Woodward, Kenneth with King, Patricia. "When a Pastor Turns Seducer" in *Newsweek*, August 28, 1989, pp. 48, 49.